TRAPUNTO

and Other Forms of Raised Quilting

TRAPUNTO
and Other Forms of Raised Quilting

MARY MORGAN and DEE MOSTELLER

illustrations by Mary Morgan/photographs by Dee Mosteller

CHARLES SCRIBNER'S SONS   NEW YORK

To my mother, who surrounded me with beauty.
To my husband, who surrounded me with love and encouragement
and whose patience through days of stitching and designing was never ending...
and with thanks for his help and advice in many of the project instructions.

Mary Morgan

To my mom and dad,
who always knew I could write a book.
And to Stephan Wilkinson, who made me do it.

Dee Mosteller

Library of Congress Cataloging in Publication Data

Morgan, Mary, 1923-
    Trapunto and other forms of raised quilting.

    Bibliography: p. 217
    1. Trapunto.   I. Mosteller, Dee, joint author.
II. Title.
TT835.M68   746.4'6   76-26180
ISBN 0-684-14821-8

1 3 5 7 9 11 13 15 17 19 MD/C 20 18 16 14 12 10 8 6 4 2

Printed in the United States of America

Contents

1. Traditional pineapple design, adapted and worked on cotton velveteen by Mary Morgan.

An Introduction to Trapunto

trapunto *n., pl.* **-tos.** quilting having an embossed design produced by outlining the pattern with single stitches and then padding it with yarn or
cotton [<It: embroidery as adj., embroidered, lit., pricked through (ptp.
of *tranpungere*), equiv. to *tra-* (<L *tra-*, var. of *trans-* TRANS-) +
-punto <L *punct*(*us*), equiv. to *pung-* (s. of *pungere* to prick) + *-tus*
ptp. suffix; see PUNCTURE]
—RANDOM HOUSE *Dictionary of the English Language* (1967)

Trapunto, an old and beautiful needlecraft adapted to modern textile arts, is an
essentially decorative quilting technique in which designs are created on fabrics
by raising them into dramatic three-dimensional figures. This is, perhaps, the only
indisputable definition we can apply to trapunto; for there are many ways to raise
a design, and their origins have melted together into obscurity. Many quilting
experts disagree as to exactly what raising techniques are encompassed by the
term "trapunto." Does it include *all* methods of raising, or does each have a distinct
meaning and function?

Based on the sketchy facts available from history and contemporary quilting
usages as well, we have allowed each basic technique its own identity. For the sake
of simplicity, when elements common to the whole body of techniques are being
described, all raised quilting is referred to as "trapunto." When dealing with one
specific type of raising, however, it is called by its own name. For those of you
who do not agree with our definitions, remember that no matter what you call it,
the end result is the same: an exciting, tactile piece of needlecraft art. The elusive-

1

ness of its origins, as a matter of fact, seems only to add to its desirability as a highly creative and individualistic handcraft.

To understand trapunto (pronounced "trā-pōōn-toe"), it is helpful first to understand its ancestor, quilting. Basically, quilting consists of two layers of material, normally with a layer of padding sandwiched in between them, all sewn together by stitches that sometimes constitute a design. This is commonly called wadded quilting. (When the center layer of padding is omitted, it is usually called flat quilting.) In standard quilting, the design is enhanced by the shadows that play in the little valleys formed where the stitches depress the padding.

In trapunto, normally only two layers of material—a top fabric and a coarsely woven backing—are used, and the designs are defined by hills, or raised areas, as well as valleys. As in standard quilting, the layers are sewn together and designs are created by the stitches. The raised portions are formed by making holes in the backing and stuffing the outlined design areas with a filler material. The stitches hold the filler in place, within the outlined areas, between the two layers of material. The effect is one of high relief, and the lights and shadows are even more pronounced and more beautiful than in regular quilting. Trapuntoed designs literally come alive, standing out in three dimensions from flat backgrounds.

This, then, is what we refer to as true trapunto: raising designs on two layers of fabric by stuffing them with loose fill material. (For example, the pineapple in photo 1 is raised in this manner.) Another traditional method is to raise narrow designs, formed by two close, parallel rows of stitching, with filler materials such as yarn or cording. This is generally known as Italian quilting. In this book it is referred to by that name and sometimes also as cording. (Italian quilting is used on the ship in photo 2.) A design can be raised by attaching a cord to the underside of a single layer of material, too, and this is also called cording. One modern trapunto

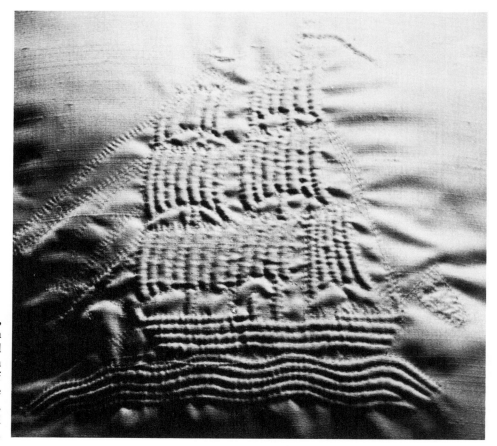

2. Corded sailing ship, done in running stitch on pongee. Design adapted from an early American petticoat in the Museum of the Daughters of the American Revolution, Washington, D.C., worked by Mary Morgan.

adaptation is raising appliqués (like the elephant in photo 3), which had its beginnings not only in raised quilting but also in embroidered "stump work" as well. Other adaptations include raising designs on pre-designed fabrics, as was done on the pillow in photo 4; and borrowing the middle layer of padding from wadded quilting to create even more prominent depressions in stuffed work and to give the piece a softer feel. Often more than one method is used on a piece.

There are many varieties of raising techniques, stitches, fabrics, and designs which can be used in trapunto, alone or in combination, and the purpose of this book is to introduce some of these options to the modern needleworker—quilter, embroiderer, and seamstress alike, for it is an extension of all these crafts. Both ancient and contemporary techniques are given, with adaptations to modern uses and materials. The do-it-yourself projects included in pages 132–209 afford practical applications for all these various methods. Some projects will seem to bear little resemblance to traditional quilting, but the basic elements are there.

The chapters in this book will teach you the basic techniques of raising and stitching; give you guides for fabric choices; and, we hope, provide inspiration for original designs. Much thought, and space, has been devoted to such factors as design selection and fabric characteristics, for we want this book in the main to encourage you to use your imagination and to adapt these instructions to your own tastes. Trapunto leaves a great deal of room for individuality and creativity. It can be done by hand or machine; with a simple or complex stitch; on cotton or silk, organza or burlap. It can have a modern look or a feeling of tradition. It can be plain or fancy. It can be delicate or bold.

Most of all, it can be fun.

—MARY MORGAN
—DEE MOSTELLER

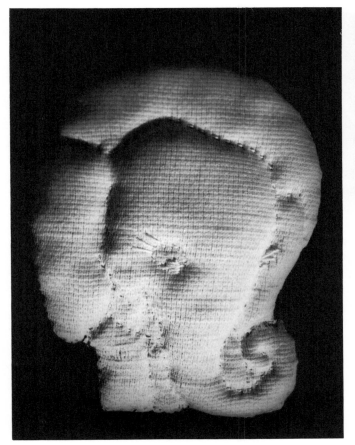

3. LEFT: Raised appliquéd elephant of heavy satin fabric . Design by Patricia Landmann for the "1975 June Fete" of the Medical Center at Princeton.

4. ABOVE: Trapunto pillow of pre-designed glazed chintz. Stuffed, quilted in running stitch, by Mary Morgan.

Definitions

The following definitions are applicable to the instructions given, and techniques used, in this book.

Appliqué: A design, or part of a design, cut from material and attached to another, larger piece of fabric with blind stitches.

Back: The bottom layer of a finished piece (pillow, quilt, pincushion, etc.), which will be seen.

Backing: A fabric, usually of coarse weave, which is stitched to the underneath side of the top fabric to hold fill materials in place. (Fill is added to design areas through holes cut in backing.) In mounting a wall hanging, the backing is a solid, stiff material (usually cardboard, Masonite, or such) over which the quilted piece is stretched and attached.

Batting: A "sheet" of fill material, sometimes used as a middle layer of insulation between the top layer and backing, for warmth or softness. Also used as fill to raise large design areas.

Block: A square of fabric, or fabrics, used as part of an overall piece. In appliqué, it is used as ground for attaching appliqués. In quilting, it is a unit, made up of top fabric and backing (and optional middle layer of padding), to be attached to other blocks to form a whole quilt.

Bodkin: A blunt needle with large eye, for cording.

Cord: The material used in cording (yarn, cable cord, or any other narrow material used to raise channel designs).

Cording: The process of raising a design by threading a cord through stitched channels, between a top fabric and backing. (Sometimes cording is attached to the back of a single layer of fabric.) Also a term applied to cording materials.

Cut-backing stuffing: The process of stuffing fill into the design area through a hole cut in the backing material.

Fill: A polyester or cotton material, either in loose fibers or sheets of batting, used to raise designs by stuffing or padding.

Filler: Any material—fill or cord—used to raise designs.

4

Flat quilting: Quilting on two layers of fabric, without batting or raised designs.

Grid: A paper divided into equal-size squares, for enlarging and reducing designs.

Ground quilting: Stitching in various patterns used to fill in the flat background around raised designs.

Italian quilting: The process of raising a design by threading a cord through a stitched channel design; same as "cording."

Open-weave stuffing: The process of stuffing fill into a design area through a hole created in the backing by pushing the fibers of the fabric apart with a pointed instrument, without breaking them, and closing them after raising is complete.

Padding: The process of raising a design by inserting a layer of batting between top fabric and backing, stitching around the design outline, and tearing or cutting away batting left outside the stitching.

Quilting: The process of sewing the layers of fabric together with stitches that outline a design; in the case of raised quilting, also to hold the fill or cord in place between the layers.

Raised quilting: Any quilting technique in which designs are raised by adding filler to the design areas enclosed by stitches, between a top fabric and backing (or on the back of a single layer).

Shadow quilting: Raised quilting in which the top fabric is semi-transparent, so that filler and backing can be seen through it.

Stuffing: The process of raising a design by inserting fill between the top fabric and backing within the stitched outline of the design.

Template: Pattern made of stiff material, such as cardboard, used in design transfer and pattern making.

Top fabric: Top layer of fabric of a piece, which will be seen.

Trapunto: Quilting technique done on two layers of fabric (top and backing), in which a design is outlined with stitches, a hole made in backing, and loose fill inserted to raise the design.

Wadded quilting: Quilting on three layers (top, middle layer of batting, backing).

5. The "Sicilian Quilt," depicting the story of Tristan. Sicilian, circa 1400.

Trapunto Yesterday, Today

ORIGINS

A textile craft is fragile, its substance vulnerable to every facet of its environment, from the elements in the air to the touch of human hands. It is difficult to trace the history of any needlecraft, for few samples survive time and wear; and quilting is no exception. Our earliest remaining example was sewn in the late fourteenth century, yet there is evidence of quilting in the more "substantial" art forms of carving and painting done several thousand years ago. The history of trapunto quilting, therefore, is woven from pieces of recorded history and from a bit of supposition as well.

The first signs of quilting are found in the antiquities of Far and Mid-Eastern countries—China, Egypt, India, Persia (Iran), and others. An ivory statue of a Pharaoh, believed to have been carved before 3000 B.C., for example, shows the Egyptian ruler wearing a royal quilted robe.

It's a fairly safe assumption to say that quilting sprang from necessity. Peasants seeking protection from the cold discovered that they could stay warmer by covering themselves with clothes or bed covers made of two layers of material sewn together with padding in between. Eventually people turned to quilting for protection from another enemy—man. One of the first uses of quilting found in Europe is in the heavily padded and quilted armor worn from the eleventh through the fifteenth centuries. The needlecraft had spread slowly from the East, borne by Crusaders and merchants who opened the Oriental trade routes. The middle layer of padding was omitted in the warmer European countries for obvious reasons; and, at some point, possibly around the end of the fourteenth century, a totally new concept of quilting was born.

The best estimate is that raised quilting began on the Mediterranean island of Sicily. Just as standard quilting grew out of practical needs, trapunto and subsequent forms of raised quilting developed as decoration for the garments and furnishings of the wealthier classes.

The oldest "living" examples of quilting (of any type) are a trio of Sicilian quilts dated circa 1392. These probably were made to be used as bed covers, but they are so ornately decorated they could easily have been wall hangings as well.

7

6. Detail of the "Sicilian Quilt."

A wedding gift for two of Sicily's aristocracy, Pietro di Luigi Guicciandi and Laodamia Acciaiuli, the quilts were elaborately covered with scenes from the legend of Tristan. (Photo 5 shows one of the three pieces in its entirety, and photo 6 is a closer view of some of the designs.)

Like most of the quilted pieces that remain from the next hundred years or so, the Sicilian quilts were made of a double layer of heavy, pieced linen and sewn with linen thread in a back stitch. The three pieces were unusual in that many of the design figures were stuffed in such a manner as to create a relief effect similar to other art forms of the time. The principal figures of people and animals were outlined with brown thread, to contrast with the natural linen fabric. This also gave them more emphasis than the secondary figures of leaves and stems which were worked in natural-colored threads. Designs were raised from the back with tiny pieces of cotton padding, and small details were stitched after the stuffing was complete. This may have been the first use of what we now call trapunto.

7. Quilt of linen, quilted with linen thread and corded. German, sixteenth century.

Two of the quilts were obviously a pair, with complementary scenes from the legend. The one shown here is at the Victoria and Albert Museum in London; the other is at the Bargello in Florence. The third piece, which was made by the same techniques, and most likely by the same artist, is in a private collection in Florence.

There is not much fifteenth-century quilting left. Literary references, however, indicate that by then in Europe quilting was done on garments, as well as bed furnishings and armor, both for reasons of comfort and as a fashion. Stuffed quilting was probably being copied from the Sicilian techniques in other countries, particularly Germany and England. Legendary characters and animals and geometric figures, embellished with floral patterns, were used in most of the designs of the time. A new technique, called ground quilting, was developed as a device for enhancing designs—both flat and raised. The flat areas around the designs were filled in with stitching in various patterns to make the designs stand out even more.

The Sixteenth Century

These techniques carried over into the sixteenth century, and patterns, fabrics, and quilting uses and methods became even more diverse and elaborate. From this period we find the first example of designs raised with cord, or strips of material. (It is possible, however, that cording developed before stuffing.) The cording was done on two layers of fabric, with narrow channels sewn and then filled from the back. This technique is now known as Italian quilting, which is perhaps a misnomer, for some sources attribute it to Portuguese quilters, while others refer to it as English.

The sixteenth-century German quilt in photo 7 is typical of the work of the period. The design consists of a series of octagons and diamonds, outlined by narrow raised channels. Within each of the geometric patterns is a fabulous beast.

The animals inside the large octagons are also surrounded by eight-point stars. Worked on two layers of linen, the designs were outlined with linen thread in a back stitch, and then a running stitch was used in a ground quilting pattern to heighten the effects of both the raised and flat designs.

Linens appear to have been used almost exclusively in early European quilting of all types. In the fifteenth and sixteenth centuries, however, various wools and cottons were introduced. Beginning in the sixteenth century, such "exotic" materials as Persian silk, lute-string, taffeta, and satin were brought by traders from the East to European quilting. Backing materials were of fustian and twilled cotton, as well as linen; and later, sarcenet and cendal, two soft, fine silks, were used as lining and backing for quilted garments. It wasn't until the nineteenth and twentieth centuries that such materials as muslin and homespun were used as backing for raised work.

Padding and stuffing in early pieces were normally of cotton, wool, or flax. Wool padding and stuffing were often soaked in vinegar to prevent iron rust and vermin infection in quilted armor . . . and, perhaps, to keep evil spirits away. Thin strands of wool and cotton were used for cording throughout the many years this technique was in vogue.

The sixteenth century was the harbinger of the importance quilting would have in the next two hundred years. New fabrics and beautiful decorative threads were introduced; suddenly "fancy" quilting began to appear on the jackets, doublets, waistcoats, caps, gowns, and petticoats of the fashionable and the wealthy. (The labor involved and the cost of the high-quality fabrics and threads were too much for the poor.) Corded quilting came into its own under the reign of the Tudor family, who popularized it by wearing quilted clothes themselves. Natural subject

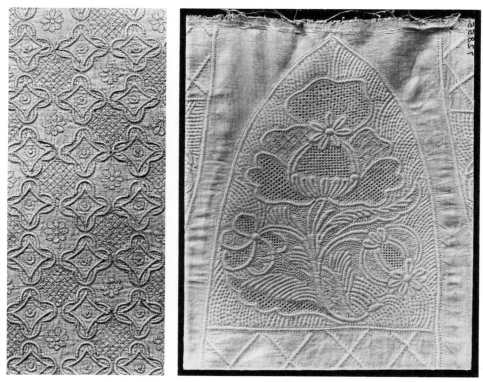

8. LEFT: Part of a robe of linen quilted with linen thread in cross-over back stitch over cord, single layer of fabric, with diamond ground quilting in back stitch. English, late seventeenth century.

9. RIGHT: Panel from a cap of linen quilted with linen thread in back and running stitches; designs are corded. English, early eighteenth century.

patterns grew more intricate and elegant; and many of the traditional designs still used in quilting today, such as the rose, fern, beehive, feather, and diamond, came out of this period.

The Seventeenth and Eighteenth Centuries

The seventeenth and early eighteenth centuries were the heyday of decorative quilting in Europe. Wadded quilting was still primarily the property of the peasants, but corded and stuffed work embellished the clothes, bed furnishings, wall hangings, and household items of the wealthy. In those days, quilting could be found in great profusion on practically everything that touched the lives of the gentry, from underwear to upholstery. Pillow cases, bed covers, valances, chairs, couches, cabinets, and chests were ornamented with corded and stuffed quilting.

Again, royalty advanced quilting by their own acceptance of it as the predominant fashion of the day. The Stuart rulers, especially James I, Charles I, Mary II, and Anne, fancied and wore elaborate quilted clothes; and Queen Mary was a quilter herself.

More fabrics were introduced to quilting; colored and metallic threads became popular; and new decorative techniques were developed. Ground quilting was used more than ever, in many patterns, such as the diamond design on the late seventeenth-century robe in photo 8, and the running stitch done in parallel lines on the cap panel in photo 9. Some pieces, like the seventeenth-century Portuguese coverlet in photo 10, were so heavily corded that there was no need for additional ground quilting or other decoration. Cording on one layer of material is first found in pieces from this era; for example, the robe in photo 8 was

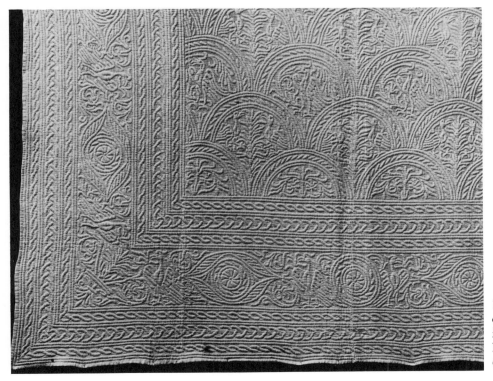

10. Coverlet of cotton, quilted with cotton thread in running stitch. Portuguese, seventeenth century.

done on a single layer of linen, using a cross-over back stitch to hold the cording in place on the back of the fabric. Italian quilting became sharper and bolder, and a technique for cording on two layers of reversible silk fabrics was developed.

Not content to stop with the basic quilting techniques developed up to that point, needleworkers began to use more involved embroidery stitches to enhance quilted work. Two particularly interesting techniques are drawn fabric, in which tiny holes are created in the piece by the stitches, and the French knot. The way

11. Dress of yellow satin quilted with yellow silk thread in back stitch. English, mid-eighteenth century.

these techniques were used with raised quilting can be seen on the cap panel in photo 9. This piece is practically a sampler of all quilting methods of the period. It has both stuffed and corded designs; ground quilting in parallel lines and diamond patterns; the two basic quilting stitches—the running and back stitches—and the two popular embroidery methods mentioned here.

It was also during these two centuries that another intriguing raised needle art became fashionable, both in England and on the Continent. Given the rather graceless name "stump work," the technique involved the use of layers of embroidery stitches, one on top of another, to build relief figures on fabric, normally white satin. To bring certain important design elements, such as human bodies and flowers, into even higher relief, sometimes tiny wooden molds were placed behind the stitching. Stump work was made even more elaborate than raised quilting by the addition of colorful "overlays" done in a variety of stitches. Complex scenes depicted plants, animals, and stars; people working, playing, planting gardens, and so forth; one French gown even supported an entire orchestra, *en symphonie!*

Stump work had many parallels with trapunto. It was done on fashionable garments and all manner of furnishings, such as side panels on jewelry and letter boxes, on frames around mirrors, in small box frames, and inside cabinets. Like trapunto, there is some question as to the derivation of its name and techniques. And also like trapunto, its popularity ended with the eighteenth century in Europe, followed by a brief vogue in American needlework. This technique is mentioned here since it is one of the influences on certain types of contemporary raised work, including embroidery and stuffed appliqués.

Quilting declined in armor, probably because the weaponry of the day could too easily penetrate a fabric shield, but it became a virtual must in fashion. Men's jackets, vests and waistcoats, caps and cloaks were richly and boldly decorated, usually by a combination of quilting methods. Women's petticoats, jackets, waistcoats, caps, and even whole dresses were equally lavish, as can be seen in the resplendent satin dress in photo 11. Even children's clothing, which would soon be outgrown, came in for its share of quilted decoration. (Fancy a modern woman making a cap like the one in photo 12 for her growing child! Of course, in that day, children's clothes were almost always handed down.)

The complexity of these pieces is almost staggering. Because of the intricacy of the work, and the consequent tedium, it was usually relegated to ladies in waiting, peasants, or professional quilters. As you might imagine, the skill and labor and the quality of the materials made each of these quilted fashions extremely dear.

The eighteenth century began as a carefree, prosperous one, but in mid-century, the socioeconomic situation began to change. The first sign of transition evident in quilting was that elaborately quilted sections were cut out of worn clothing and saved to be sewn onto new garments. Fabrics were changing, too, becoming too thin to support heavy quilting. New dress styles and printed fabrics not conducive to the quilting techniques of the day were growing more popular. Quilting as a decorative needlework began to diminish in England and on the Continent in the last half of the century.

Trapunto in American History

As the craft waned in England, however, it started to rise in America. Quilting had been brought to the colonies in the seventeenth century by English and

12. Child's cap of white cotton quilted with white linen thread and decorated with French knot embroidery work. English, early eighteenth century.

Dutch settlers, but regulations imposed by the mother country limited the needlecraft in the early days. Before 1640, for example, all fabrics had to be brought from England, a regulation designed to support British industry. After that date, when fabrics came into short supply, the colonists were allowed, even encouraged, to make their own fabrics. Eventually, a rule was made to the effect that each colonial family had to have one member who was a full-time spinner. This was usually a child or an unmarried woman (hence the term "spinster").

During the colonial period, American quilting was primarily a copy of English and Continental techniques, somewhat simplified to meet the needs of settling a new world. During the revolutionary era, American sympathies and tastes turned more toward the French; and finally, in the frontier days, American quilting began to acquire its own style with the development of the patchwork quilt. Because fabrics were dear, no scrap was wasted. Every inch of material was saved until there were enough to build a quilt, bit by tiny bit. Patchwork was another daughter of necessity, but it developed into an extremely diverse and beautiful craft, until today it is considered to be a major art form.

After the revolutionary period, quilting became more than just an economic necessity. It gave the homemaker a chance to be creative and to add a little color to the drabness of a crude home; a way to sit quietly alone, or chatting with friends, without suffering the guilt of idleness. The introduction of the quilting frame in the mid-1700s further encouraged the craft as a group effort and supplied a tangible bond for neighboring needleworkers.

Raised quilting had been borrowed from Europe in the early days of settlement, for use on a few choice pieces of clothing and bed coverings; but it was not until America was a bit more sure of its status as a nation, and true "refinement" had come to the older northeastern states, that quilters had the time and desire to add such embellishments as stuffed and corded designs. Once again, trapunto became a craft of the wealthy and the leisurely. It was done in urban parlors by young ladies whose future lives would revolve around genteel homemaking; and some of the most beautiful uses of raised quilting ever developed came out of this era.

It was during this time that raised quilting reached a peak of beauty and effectiveness in the all-white quilt. This was done by stitching elaborate designs on white fabrics with white thread that was almost invisible on the background, relying solely on the lights and shadows of the raised areas to emphasize the design. All-white work was also done in England during the late eighteenth century, but by the time it realized its great popularity, quilting was passé in Britain.

The white counterpane in photo 13 is an early example of all-white quilting at its best. Made of muslin with a homespun backing, it has an elaborate design of fruit and flowers, which incorporates two well-known patterns, the "Tree of Life" and the "Princess Feather." A circular central motif is the focal point of the piece. Designs were outlined with a running stitch and cotton was added through the backing to raise them.

A slightly later all-white cotton batiste quilt done by Jane Voorhees (photo 14) shows how vastly different these quilts could appear. The Voorhees quilt has much larger, bolder, and more heavily padded designs, and they are further enhanced by parallel lines of cording which run diagonally across all the areas of the quilt that would otherwise have been left flat. In other words, the cording took the place of ground quilting. Jane Voorhees added another interesting touch to her

13. All-white counterpane of muslin with homespun backing, stuffed with cotton.
Made by Marie Washington Layfield Miller. American, circa 1820.

14. All-white quilt of cotton batiste, by Jane Voorhees. American, 1830–31.

quilt: the date of its creation (1830/31) and her name. She was rightfully proud of the skill and time she expended to create this true work of art.

All-white crib quilts were simply smaller versions of the standard-size counterpanes and were popular as christening gifts in the nineteenth century.

White work designs, like those in other media of the period, reflected the nineteenth-century revival of Greco-Roman motifs: floral and leaf designs, cornucopias, feathers, medallions, and diamond roping. They were generally done on cotton or muslin; and because there was no middle layer of padding they were of little practical use. Instead, they were display pieces; the very fine handwork that is evident in them shows that the needlecrafters were conscious that their work would be viewed as art. Even the stuffing was done by separating the fibers of the backing with a stiletto or needle, so that one would be hard-pressed to find where the openings were made.

Elaborate quilted pieces were often made in celebration of some special occasion, like a wedding or a fair. In those days, it was traditional for young women with even the vaguest prospects of marriage to sew thirteen quilts as the start of their future household furnishings. The first twelve were practical wadded pieces, soft and warm to sleep beneath. The final quilt was the *pièce de résistance*. It was beautiful, and somewhat impractical, and the work displayed both the creative abilities of the young woman (was this, perhaps, an advertisement to her future husband?) and many of the quilting techniques used in that day. These were often all-white works with raised designs, although appliquéd hearts and flowers were also a popular device for wedding quilts.

Show quilts also often utilized raised quilting because of the striking appearance it gave the designs. It seems logical to assume that the white quilt in photos 15 and 16 was made for a country fair, as it depicts scenes of a fairground near Russellville, Kentucky, in 1856. The artist, Virginia Ivey, probably spent more than a year doing the thousands of tiny stitches and hundreds of stuffed areas that went into this masterpiece. We hope she won first prize!

America passed its first hundred years as an independent nation, and Old World influences faded more and more. Quilting designs and techniques became more indigenous to this country. Patchwork developed into something of an American folk art, and combination quilts became popular. The mid-nineteenth-century quilt in photo 17, for example, was done with pieced, appliquéd, raised, and ground quilting. It also displayed some of the best-known designs of the day: a wide "Princess Feather" border, "Crown" appliqués, diamond and wine-glass ground quilting motifs within the appliqué centers, and a sawtooth border.

Designs were no longer simply copied from European patterns. They began to reflect the important social changes that the country was going through. Religion was vital to Americans during the eighteenth and nineteenth centuries, so religious figures appeared in the needlework of the day. During the centennial years, patriotic motifs, like the stars and stripes and eagle in the quilt shown in photos 18 and 19, were naturally in style.

Raised quilting was used for garments and household furnishings to some extent, but never as much as in Europe. Petticoats, dressing gowns, jackets, the collars and cuffs of shirts and blouses, and such items as bureau covers, pillowcases, valances, and other bed furnishings were sometimes decorated with stuffed or corded designs.

Trapunto in America was normally done on lighter fabrics, such as cotton. In the early days, of course, the fabrics were all hand-woven and homespun, and

15. ABOVE: **All-white quilted counterpane, by Virginia Ivey. American, 1856. Inscription around central design reads: "1856 A Representation of the Fair Ground Near Russellville, Kentucky."**

16. RIGHT: Detail of counterpane in photo 15.

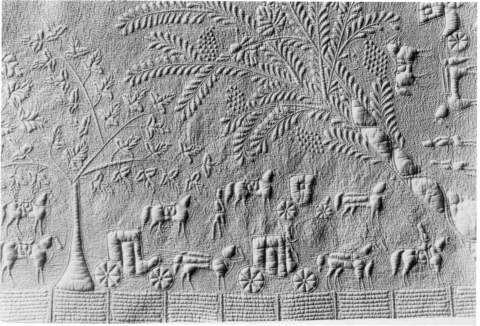

17. Pieced-work quilt (padded), in crown pattern with sawtooth borders. Made by Mrs. Mary Lawson Ruth McCrea (initialed and dated). American, 1860.

19. RIGHT: Detail of quilt in photo 18.

18. BELOW: "Rose of Sharon" appliqué quilt with stuffed designs. American, third quarter nineteenth century.

they were fairly simple. During the Industrial Revolution, however, factory-made fabrics of all types worked their way into American quilting. Backings were usually of coarsely woven cotton.

Cotton was also the predominant material used to raise designs in traditional American quilting. Normally it was rolled into very small elongated "balls" between the thumb and forefinger and pushed through minute holes in the backing one by one until the area was raised. (You can observe this method in some old American quilts by holding them up to a strong light.) American quilters, however, have always had a great deal of imagination when it comes to the stuffing. Handcrafters, with great inventiveness, or out of necessity, have used straw, feathers, wood chips and shavings, seeds, weeds, cane, flannel, lint, and all sorts of fabric scraps to raise designs. Cording was usually long, thin strands of wool or cotton, although sometimes candlewick or other cord was used.

Quilting remained in fashion in America until the latter part of the 1800s. The Industrial Revolution had made its mark, however, particularly with the invention of the sewing machine, which did little to encourage handcraft. People's lives changed significantly, and so did their interest in such occupations as needlework. There were more amusements, and more outside work, to lure a woman from her house and less time for her to sit and stitch. Practical quilting has never quite died out, but decorative quilting, such as stuffed and corded work, disappeared except for an occasional novelty piece.

By the twentieth century, most of the sewing in Europe and America was being done on machines. In the late 1920s and early 1930s there was a revival of all types of quilting in England and Wales as a cottage industry grew up to supplement incomes during the coal-mining depression. Once again, quilting began to decorate household goods, christening jackets, baby blankets, dressing gowns, lounging jackets, bodices, trim for collars and cuffs, and cushions. But it was on a much smaller, less grand scale than before.

In America there was also a brief flare-up of corded quilting during that time. Such feminine articles as lingerie and lingerie boxes, satin pillows, dressing gowns and slippers, and other bedroom accessories were decorated with simple, beautiful designs raised by cording. From time to time since then, trapunto has appeared on clothing and furnishings, only to die down again.

In the 1960s, in both Britain and America, a different sort of rebirth began. Slowly and steadily, all types of old handcrafts were revived and new ones began to develop. And now begins an era of extremely exciting needlecraft.

CONTEMPORARY TRAPUNTO

In recent years, people have experienced a great desire to get away from factory-made things, and to learn, or relearn, to handcraft clothes, furnishings, and many other items, both practical and esoteric. Artists seeking fresh media for their work have turned to textiles and needlework for various forms of art. During this revival, quilting of all types is once again enjoying a period of popularity. Quilted pieces are *objets d'art* now, hung in galleries and displayed all over the world. Clothes are quilted both for warmth and for style; household furnishings are dressed up with unique quilted effects. And raised quilting has come in for its share of attention, exciting the imagination of modern needlecrafters and textile artists alike.

Today's trapunto is compatible with the relative simplicity of modern life: a single large, graceful butterfly on a long velvet evening skirt; a contemporary

20. "Untitled I," wall hanging by Sandra Hanson. Top fabric of synthetic knit, backing of unbleached muslin. Cut-backing stuffing with polyester fill; machine stitching. (Photo by Doug Bauman)

21. "Faces," soft sculpture by Norma Minkowitz. Crocheted, stuffed. (Photo courtesy of Kobler/Dyer Studio)

22. Purse of unbleached muslin, raised with cording and padded with polyester batting. Designed and worked by Mary Morgan; purse pattern from McCall's (No. 4613).

23. "Face" pillow by Shari Erickson. Organdy top fabric, dark-colored polyester/cotton blend backing. Hand-stitched, stuffed with polyester fill. (Photo courtesy of the artist)

Chinese design on the detachable yoke and cuffs of a washable caftan; or a simple corded design turning a plain little dress into a unique piece of needlework. Sports scenes are raised on jackets, golf shirts and skirts, tennis togs and racket covers. Monograms are corded on collars, cuffs, and pockets of shirts, dresses, blouses, and jackets. Appliqués are stuffed on faded blue jeans; corded spiderwebs are spun on the back of inexpensive workshirts or blouses, airplanes are raised on purses.

In the home, trapunto is used to soften and dress a chair back or seat, the bottom of curtains, dresser and bed ruffles, and decorator pillows. Quilts and coverlets are still being decorated with raised designs, but rarely as elaborately or as often as before. In the kitchen, pot holders and hot mitts, place mats; aprons, and covers for mixers, toasters, blenders, and teapots have raised designs taken from china patterns, cookie cutters, salt boxes, and linoleum floor coverings.

Trapunto has become a hobby with practical purposes for men and women, even simplified enough for children and beginning sewers, and a viable business venture for craftspeople.

And artists have adapted trapunto to all types of materials, for jewelry, wall hangings, and soft sculpture.

Gone are most of the inhibitions as to choice of fabric, design, raising techniques, and stitches. Needlecrafters are raising designs on burlap with styrofoam stuffing and others are doing creative stitching on sewing machines. And they are proving that the traditional methods are as exciting as ever.

Raised quilting is now truly the property of every needlecrafter.

24. LEFT: Neckpiece by Irene C. Reed. Figures of nylon mesh, borders crocheted. Machine stitched; stuffed with polyester fill.

25. CENTER: "12 Tribes," wall hanging by Bucky King. White-on-white, linens and cotton. Trapunto and cutwork, with drawn and pulled embroidery. (Photo courtesy of the artist)

26. RIGHT: "Richmond Farm House," soft sculpture by Robin E. Muller (18 inches high). Yellow satin, seed beads, and gold braid. Individual panels quilted and stuffed separately, padded with batting. (Photo courtesy of Thiel Studio)

27. Batiked birds by Cynthia King. Cotton was batiked by the artist, machine stitched, and stuffed.

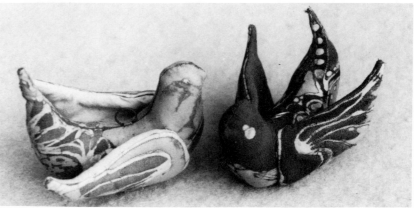

28. LEFT: "Midnight Rainbow, Morning Starshine," soft sculpture by Joan A. Blumenbaum. Female image silk-screened on silver knit fabric, machine embroidered, stitched to organdy backing, and stuffed. Cloud formation machine stitched (satin stitch) to organdy and stuffed; circle appliquéd to cloud. Rainbow effect created by varicolored velvet appliqués. Polyester fill used for stuffed areas, polyester batting added to quilted areas. (Photo courtesy of the artist)

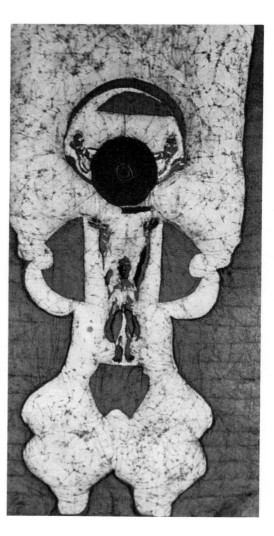

29. ABOVE: "Stained Glass Quilt," by Robin E. Muller (45 inches in diameter). Violet, burgundy, and blue no-wale corduroy and bright red velveteen. Appliquéd, machine quilted, raised with batting. Muslin backing. (Photo courtesy of Thiel Studio)

30. RIGHT: "Yin," soft sculpture/wall hanging by Rita Shumaker. Batiked cotton, fur, and suede cloth, with peacock feather. Quilted in running stitch, stuffed with polyester fill. Cotton backing. (Photo courtesy of the artist)

31. LEFT: "Woman Is a Branched Tree," wall hanging by Berni Gorski. Hand quilted in stem (outline) stitch and buttonhole stitch. Cotton with loosely woven backing. Cut-backing stuffing with polyester fill. Figures stuffed and appliquéd. Title from Irish folk song, "Rue." (Photo by Andrew Skolnick)

32. ABOVE: Child's dress by Mary Morgan. Open-weave stuffing and cording on two layers.

33. BELOW: Sleeping bag/wall hanging by Norma Minkowitz. Crocheted, knitted, quilted, appliquéd, and stuffed. From Museum of Contemporary Crafts' show, "Portable World." (Photo by Bob Hanson)

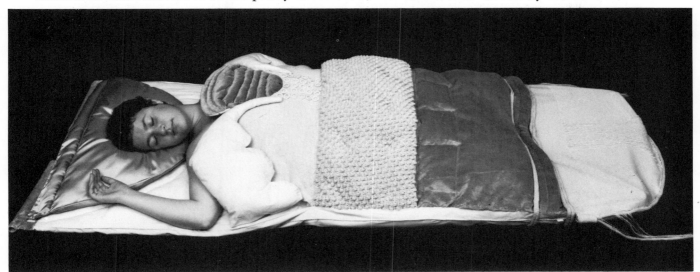

Fabrics and Tools

FABRICS

The fabrics you choose for raised quilting can make or break your project. That's how important it is to select materials compatible with the objective of trapunto—to produce a design that is defined more by the "hills" of the raised areas and the "valleys" of the stitching than by tangible printed pictures and colors.

There are so many fabrics on the market today that it is impossible to name all that are suitable for raised quilting. You can raise a design on almost any fabric, unless it is too heavy to sew on or to "give" in the raising process. There are, however, some guidelines that can help you choose the best materials for the job. To show the effects of raising designs on various fabrics, the projects in this book were done on a wide variety of materials, with various techniques of raising.

This chapter deals only with the top fabric, the (optional) middle layer of padding, and the backing fabric; materials for stuffing and cording are discussed in the chapter "Raising the Design," along with the appropriate raising techniques.

The Top Fabric

Selecting a top fabric may be the hardest decision in trapunto because you have

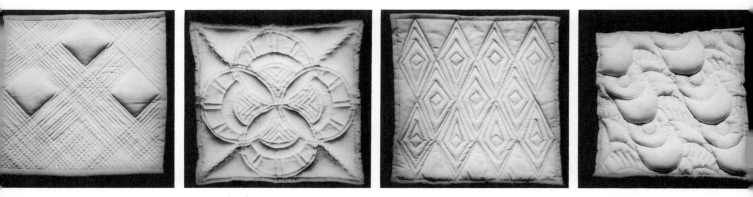

34. Art sampler pieces in original designs by the students of Marilyn Leon show the varied appearance created by different shapes and sizes of designs on the same fabric. Top and backing of unbleached muslin, all machine stitched.

so many options and so many considerations. There are five major questions to be answered, in addition to satisfying your own personal preference:

1. Is it supple? The fabric has to "give" when the extra padding or cording is added, in order to raise the design properly. The weight or thickness will determine how much give the fabric will have. Generally, a lightweight fabric, sometimes referred to as "dress weight," is a better medium for trapunto than a heavy one.

2. Is it easy to hand sew with small stitches? The weight, finish, and weave of a fabric will affect the way it handles and, consequently, the pleasure of your work. Some tightly woven or knit fabrics, for example, are hard to pull a needle through. And it's almost impossible to do a small, even running stitch—the basic quilting stitch—on a heavy fabric. If you aren't too bashful, take along a needle when you shop for material. With the permission of the salesperson (of course), do a stitch or two in a corner of the fabric. Try before you buy.

3. Will it show off the design well? The color, weave, weight, and texture of the fabric will all affect the success of the raising. A white or light-colored fabric with a smooth surface is the best combination of all, for it will reflect light and create a greater contrast with the shadows. Fabrics with a twill weave, like gabardine, and those with a surface line texture, like corduroy, can detract from a small design. These are not as well suited to raised quilting as materials with a plain (even) weave, like broadcloth and chintz, or a satin weave, like sateen and satin.

4. Is it compatible with the raising technique you have chosen? Normally, any smooth, flexible material will do well for both cording and stuffing, but some materials with a plain (even) weave, like broadcloth and chintz, or a satin are wonderful for use in stuffing, but not as strong as fine linen or cotton for corded work. Soft leather (chamois) and suede show off simple corded designs better than stuffed ones. Small design areas are best done on quite pliable fabrics.

For shadow quilting (page 121), the top piece must be at least somewhat transparent: organdy, voile, organza, fine silk or lawn, are appropriate. In appliqué stuffing (page 109), use fabrics like broadcloth and percale which will not fray easily.

5. And, finally, does the fabric suit the use of the finished piece? If the article is something that you will be using or wearing regularly, it's best to choose a fabric that is colorfast, pre-shrunk, and washable.

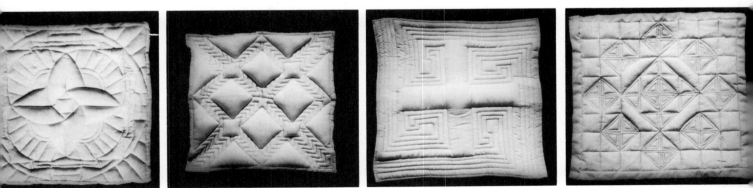

All pieces are padded with polyester batting, and all are stuffed with polyester fill, with the exception of the third photo on page 26, which is stitched only. Layer of batting gives this piece the appearance of being slightly raised.

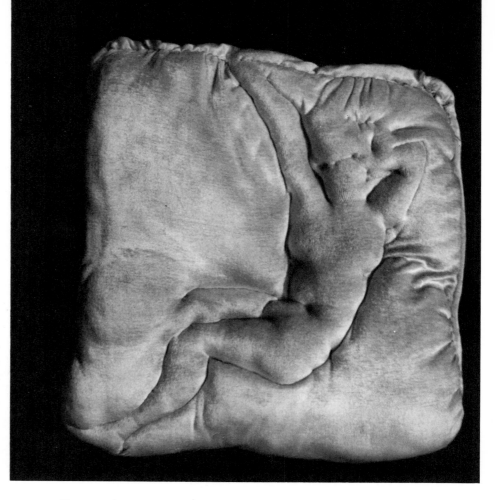

35. Human figure pillow by Marcia Shapiro. Panne velvet is an excellent example of a supple, lightweight fabric that works well with raised designs; natural stretch produces a molded effect and velvet sheen gives it the appearance of marble.

For wearing apparel, the warmth of wool, the coolness of cotton, the strength of linen, and the beauty of silk can hardly be surpassed. On the other hand, the easy care of synthetics seems to balance the scale of desirability. Wash-and-wear fabrics are ideal because ironing raised quilting is practically impossible. Just remember that all man-made fabrics are not wash-and-wear; some require dry cleaning, which can be a practical and economic factor in your choice. Check the cleaning code on the fabric bolt before you buy.

Other quilted pieces that should be able to withstand at least the "delicate" cycles of modern washing machines are coverlets and play sheets for a child's bed, pillows that will be tossed on the floor and played with, kitchen appliance covers, hot mitts, and so forth.

If the piece is going to be hung on the wall, kept under glass, or simply displayed on a drawing room sofa, the cleaning factor is not such a big one.

If you could answer yes to all five questions, the fabric you have chosen should work well on your piece.

Cottons

The cotton family includes broadcloth, chintz, corduroy, glazed chintz, India cotton, Oxford cloth, percale, poplin, sateen, unbleached muslin, and velveteen; and all but the heaviest are ideal for any type of raised quilting. Many are available blended with polyester, which adds durability, a smoother surface, and wrinkle-resis-

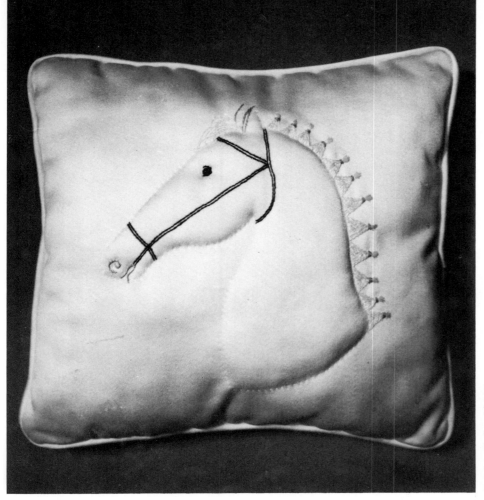

36. Horse head pillow by
Mrs. John North Caldwell.
White decorator fabric of
cotton sateen shows off
stuffed figures well.
(Pillow available through
Emily Whitmore Crewel &
Crafts)

tance—all highly desirable qualities for trapunto.

Cotton broadcloth, percale, India cotton, and a blend of unbleached muslin
and polyester, particularly, are lightweight, pretty, and effective for raised designs.
Woven broadcloth with a blend of 65 percent polyester and 35 percent cotton is
very durable, easy to sew, and has a lovely sheen.

Soft velveteens and velvets are pliable, elegant, and beautiful, and the pile
tends to hide the quilting stitches (which *can* be a blessing). The subtle lights and
shadows inherent in velvets and velveteens also enhance the dramatic effect of the
raised design. These are extremely rich-looking materials and very pleasant to feel,
as well—both suitable characteristics for a tactile craft like trapunto. Cotton velveteen has the added advantage of being washable.

Corduroy is not generally as good for trapunto work as other cottons because
its own distinct line texture tends to overpower a small quilted design. There are,
however, some new, soft cotton corduroys and corduroy/synthetic blends, with
a close wale, which produce effects similar to velvet or velveteen, though with
slightly less of the dramatic shadings.

Cotton sateen, a weave with a soft surface sheen, covers a wide span of fabrics.
Sateen lining is quite elegant in appearance but very inexpensive in price, while
other sateen fabrics cost as much as $15 a yard, wholesale. These fabrics have
much in common: they are equally easy to sew, raise well, and are fairly easy to
care for ... but they are of very different weights and prices.

37. Cotton fabrics suitable for trapunto (top row, left to right): India cotton, sateen lining, glazed chintz, crinkle cotton; (middle) satin-weave lining, lightweight cotton drapery fabric; (bottom) corduroy, polished cotton, unbleached muslin, middle-grade satin weave.

Silks

The lighter (dress) weight, cultivated silks can be choice fabrics because of their suppleness and overall exquisite appearance, but they are expensive and hard to find in solid light colors. Some of the best are crepe de chine, shantung, and pongee. China silk, often used as a lining fabric, is almost too lightweight, although it can be used for raising delicate designs. Raw silk has a rough texture that can distract from the design, and silk brocade and satin may be too heavy for raising well.

Silks are not as easy to work with, or to care for, as most of the beautiful synthetics that imitate their appearance.

Linens

Linens in a dress weight are quite good for trapunto, but the heavy, rough types are hard to sew on and do not have enough give to raise well. Handkerchief linen is very pleasant to sew and is pliable enough to raise a design without distorting the surrounding background area. Its main drawback is that it wrinkles easily. Most dress linen has been treated with a resin finish to avoid that problem.

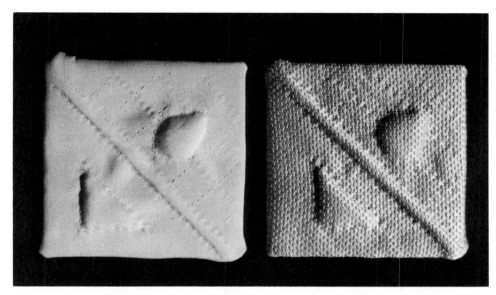

38. Silk fabrics suitable for trapunto: heavy basket-weave (right) and medium dress weight. Lighter-weight fabric shows off stuffed and corded designs better than heavy weave.

39. Linen fabrics suitable for trapunto: heavy linen (right) with buttonhole twist thread worked in back stitch to enhance design; and handkerchief linen. Lighter-weight fabric shows raised designs better than heavier piece.

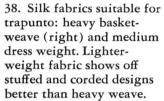

40. Wool fabrics suitable for trapunto: viyella (50 percent wool/50 percent cotton blend) and felt (right).

Wools

The wool family group offers less of a selection for raised work, and wools are not so easy to care for as other fabrics. Choose a lightweight, soft, flexible wool without a nub, deep pile, or weave pattern for best results. A wool and cotton blend called viyella is one of the best "warm" materials available for trapunto.

Man-Made Fabrics

Synthetics (materials made from coal and petroleum) which lend well to raised work are polyester, nylon, olefins, and acrylic. There are several varieties of each of these synthetics, as different manufacturers give them different properties. Some of the registered trade names, like Dacron®, Kodel®, Acrilan®, and Orlon®, have become so well known they are nearly generic terms. Many of these launder easily and never need ironing; yet they can look as elegant as the most expensive silk.

It may surprise you to know that rayon and acetate are not synthetics, because they are made from natural plant sources—wood and cotton linters. They are, instead, "cellulosic" fibers. Some rayons are not suitable for trapunto, because they have a tendency to fuzz when a thread is pulled or the fabric is cut. Acetates are better, but they are normally more effective when used as a backing material for garments than as top fabrics.

"Art" Fabrics

Modern artists and craftspeople use literally everything for raising designs. There are fascinating and exciting pieces made of burlap, crocheted materials, felt, terrycloth, batik, and copper Mylar. Soft leathers, suedes, and chamois can be very effective, although they are somewhat harder to sew because of their thickness. Chamois, especially, is an intriguing medium for trapunto, because it is fairly pliable, wonderful to feel, and relatively inexpensive compared to other leathers. Chamois is particularly appropriate for "human" art.

Things to Avoid

As was mentioned before, there are few fabrics which cannot be adapted to raised work; but there are some things to avoid if you want to keep your sanity. Poor-quality fabrics, whether natural or synthetic, will misbehave in the sewing process and rarely achieve exactly the effect you want. Other things that are especially annoying are synthetics that fuzz, fabrics that tend to unravel badly at raw edges, and cotton with sizing added to give it body. This sizing will come out in the first washing, leaving the material limp and coarse, and it is usually added only to fabrics of relatively poor quality.

Pre-Designed Fabrics

In choosing pre-designed fabrics for trapunto, the same basic guidelines apply. They should be lightweight, supple, soft, easy to sew, conducive to showing off the raised design, and cleanable, if necessary. Both dress and decorator materials are suitable, in cottons, wools, silks, satins, linens, and man-made fibers.

Backing Fabrics

A backing fabric is used to hold the material that raises the design in place and is the medium through which that material is inserted into the design areas.

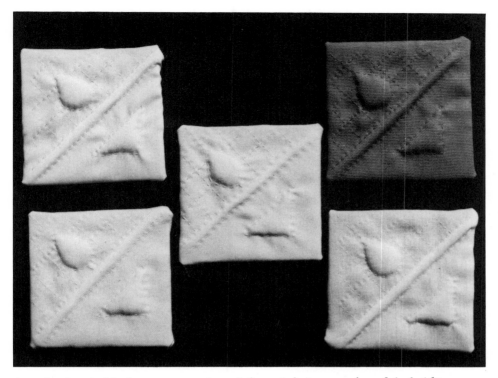

41. Blends suitable for trapunto: (top, left to right) woven broadcloth (65 percent polyester/35 percent cotton) and Super Stowe® (50 percent Kodel® polyester/50 percent cotton); (middle) poplin (65 percent Dacron®/35 percent cotton); (bottom) Oxford cloth (65 percent polyester/35 percent cotton) and muslin (polyester/cotton).

It is often of a coarse weave, because the fibers must be cut or separated to allow the stuffing or cording. The type of backing fabric you choose will depend somewhat on the method of opening the fabric for raising the design, on the use of the finished product, and, in some cases, on the weight of the top fabric.

For cut-backing stuffing (page 95), just about any cotton or synthetic fabric is suitable, even the most inexpensive ones. Unbleached muslin is especially good.

In open-weave stuffing (page 94) and cording (page 99), any fairly loosely woven fabric that will allow the separation of the fibers with a pointed instrument will work. The most important quality of the fabric is that it can be opened easily and the fibers closed after the filler material has been added. The best general backing for this purpose is a No. 120 cheesecloth, similar to diaper fabric. This is a smooth cotton with relatively coarse weave, though much finer than the cheesecloth normally used for polishing. The main drawback is that it is difficult to obtain for retail use. Loosely woven (non-crinkled) India cotton is very good and much more readily available than No. 120 cheesecloth. It can be lightly covered with spray-on starch to give it more body and make it more manageable when transferring designs and pinning or basting the fabrics together.

For pieces where the fibers must be separated and closed neatly because the backing will be seen (as on a quilt), one of the best fabrics available is a coarsely woven bed sheeting of muslin. (Percale is too closely woven for easy separation of the fibers.)

42. "Self Portrait," wall hanging by Susan Aaron-Taylor. A good example of interesting materials being used by textile artists, the piece includes copper satin, brown Swiss straw, and copper Mylar®. Done in coiled basketry, plain quilting, and trapunto. (Photo by Harry Taylor)

Special Use Backing

For garments without a lining, where the backing will be next to the skin or undergarments, a smoother, more comfortable backing should be used. A synthetic called SiBonne lining is excellent because it feels good to the wearer and moves well with the body. It will not ravel badly when cut and resewn, but it does have a tendency to slip in handling more than the others; so, it should be basted securely to the top piece with close rows of stitching 1 to 2 inches apart. SiBonne does double duty as garment liner and backing for the raised areas on the butterfly and print skirts in photos 193 and 195.

When heavier, coarse fabrics, like burlap and felt, are to be raised, the backing should be a material that has little give. Otherwise, the added padding will raise the backing instead of the top fabric! Some suitable fabrics for this use are hair canvas interfacing, multipurpose tie-shape interfacing (for neckties), and drill light-canvas-type fabric. All of these should be quilted on the sewing machine.

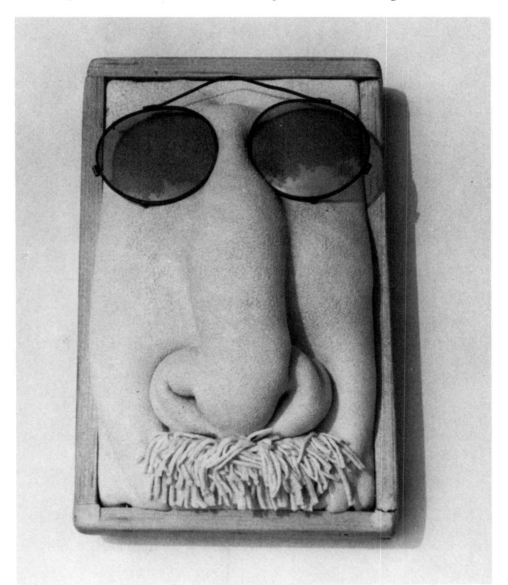

43. Wall hanging by Kathy Alcorn shows the fine flexibility of chamois leather for use in raised quilting.

The Middle Layer of Padding

In traditional trapunto and Italian quilting, there is no middle layer of padding as is used in wadded quilting, primarily because raised quilting began in warmer countries where the extra layer was not needed for warmth. Also, a flat background generally gives more emphasis to the raised areas than a padded one. There are, however, certain instances when you might want to add a layer of batting between the top and backing fabrics: for warmth in outdoor garments and bed coverings, and for more softness in such pieces as pillows, bed coverlets, and chair seats. A layer of batting was added to the tea cozy in photo 220 for insulation, and to the pillow in photo 4 for softness.

Another case where the padding might be used is on an article with many small design areas which should be raised slightly but which are hard to work with. By quilting around the designs through a layer of batting, you achieve an overall raised effect on the piece. Major design areas can then be raised even higher with extra fill to make them stand out from the rest. This is how wadded quilting gets its raised look. Sometimes it's difficult to tell if a piece with batting is raised work or not. (This technique was used in the Persian wall hanging in photo 187.)

If you decide to use a middle layer, there are basically two options for the material: polyester batting and cotton batting. Polyester is easy to care for, but it often has so much resiliency ("puff") that the main designs in a piece are almost lost among the secondary designs that have been outlined but not stuffed with extra fill. This effect can detract from the overall appearance of the piece. If there is a good deal of stitching—particularly machine stitching—on the piece, polyester batting can be flattened enough for the main design to show well. (You can see this effect on several of the sampler blocks on pages 26 and 27.)

Cotton will not launder and dry as easily, but it will give a flatter background. Old quilts, like the one in photo 79, with cotton quilt batting, sometimes look as though there were no middle layer at all, because the cotton has matted down with years and use. Designs taken from the same quilt were worked up on modern fabrics in two pieces—one without a batting (photo 44) and one with batting (photo 45) to show the striking difference the addition of this layer can make in the appearance of a raised design.

The final effect desired, and the use of the piece, will influence the decision.

Where to Find Fabrics for Trapunto

Many fabrics of cotton and cotton blends, and the more common types of backing materials, are readily available in all sewing departments and fabric shops, particularly those that cater to the dressmaker. Many stores, however, do not carry a variety of expensive silks and linens. A good selection of chintz fabrics can be found in shops where curtain and upholstery lines are carried. Quilt batting and fill are available in almost every fabric shop or sewing department and through mail order sources as well (some are included in the list of suppliers, page 211). Remnant counters are often a good source of fabrics at low cost.

If you're looking for unusual pieces, decorator shops and mill-end outlets yield a good variety of remnants, slightly irregular pieces, and discontinued fabrics, often at real bargain prices. Decorator samples, unusual and expensive in their original state, often are donated to charitable organizations for resale at bazaars and second-hand stores. The floral print skirt in photo 193 was a mill-end, which cost the author about half its original price. The Persian wall hanging in photo 187 was actually a leftover from a bolt of fabric wall covering. (The paper backing was soaked and scraped away before it was quilted—a real "find" in a back room.)

If you need a great deal of material, large fabric houses and dressmaking establishments usually sell their remnants in pound lots.

It's fun to find someone else who saves odds and ends of beautiful things—and more of a challenge to get them to give up their treasures. By using your imagination, you can find all sorts of unique materials in strange places—attics, thrift shops, auctions, and flea markets, for example. But keep in mind that, unless you plan to use them for art pieces, old, worn materials are seldom a bargain at any price—even free.

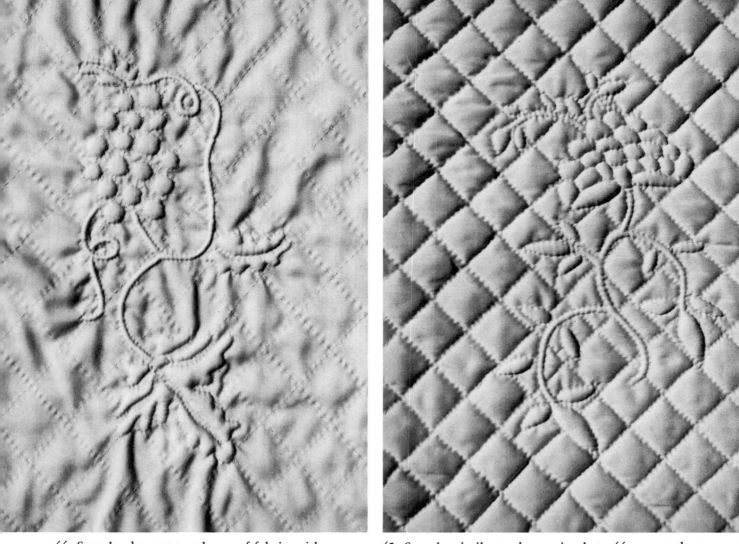

44. Sampler done on two layers of fabric, with no middle layer of batting. Design worked in running stitch, with ground quilting in diamond pattern.

45. Sampler similar to the one in photo 44, except that a middle layer of batting has been added to show the contrast in appearance the batting can make. Design worked in running stitch with diamond ground quilting. Both pieces copied from the Hock quilt in photo 79 and worked by Mary Morgan.

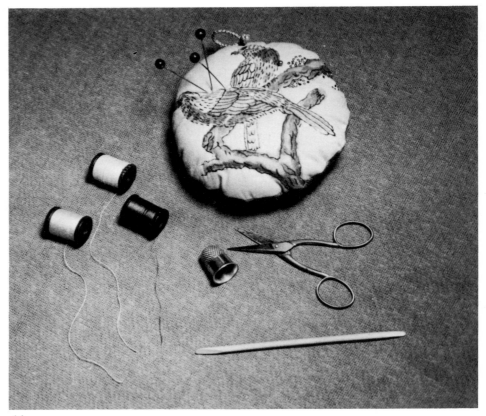

46.

BASIC TOOLS

The basic equipment used in raised quilting can be found in most homes:

Thread
Scissors
Needles
Thimble
Straight pins
Medium-lead pencils

There are other items that can make your sewing easier, like a needle-threader, but they are not necessary. For transferring designs, you'll need tracing paper, cardboard, and carbon paper, but these materials are discussed in the section on applying designs (pages 54–66.)

Thread

Almost any regular sewing thread on the market today will work satisfactorily for raised quilting, but the type you use will have an effect on both the appearance of the design and the speed and ease of your sewing. In many cases, the stitches are secondary to the design; and, therefore, the thread should match the color of the fabric, blending quietly into the background so it doesn't distract from the design.

At other times the stitches constitute a major part of the design. In such a case you might choose a heavier thread, like embroidery floss, one of a contrasting color, or one made of special materials, such as gold or silver metal, so that the stitches will stand out and be an effective design element.

There is a cotton thread made especially for quilting, which has been coated for smoother sewing and durability. Quite logically called quilting thread, it's easy to thread into the needle, pulls smoothly with little, if any, snarling, and is about the least expensive of all threads discussed here. It is available in a fairly good selection of colors in most large sewing departments and shops.

Standard mercerized cotton (No. 50) is fine, and you can do your own waxing for smoother sewing by running the thread across a piece of beeswax several times. (Good department, dime, and sewing stores carry beeswax and a tiny piece will last you for years.)

Silk threads are so smooth and light they literally fly through the fabric, and once you've tried them, you'll probably never want to use anything else again. They are, however, somewhat impractical for large quilted pieces, because of their relatively high cost (more than twice as expensive as mercerized cotton or quilting thread), or for pieces that will be washed often, because they do not launder well.

Some quilters use synthetic threads (polyester) because of their strength; others claim that they have a certain stretch that is not desirable. They do tend to knot and snarl when pulled through in hand sewing. But synthetics *are* relatively inexpensive and more readily available in a wide variety of colors than silk or cotton.

Decorative Threads

To produce truly elegant decorative stitches, try one of the beautiful gold or silver threads found in most sewing shops and craft stores. These are particularly effective for such stitches as the chain or loop, as you can see in the velvet sampler in photo 110. One problem with metallic threads is that they wear out quickly in sewing; so work with a piece no longer than 18 inches, or you'll find your thread unraveling (the outer metallic covering pulling away from the core of the thread).

A heavy silk thread called buttonhole twist produces a more visible stitch than regular silk or cotton threads and is excellent for creating interesting design effects. It is most effective when used in a back stitch or as a bobbin thread for machine stitching. For hand sewing with buttonhole twist, use a No. 8 embroidery needle and work with an 18-inch length of thread, because it unwinds or loses its twist as you sew.

Cotton embroidery floss can be used for decorative stitches also, but it is more suitable than metallic threads and silk buttonhole twist for use on less "refined" fabrics.

Whatever you use, make sure your threads are fresh and strong. Old thread will not last, either in the sewing process or in the cleanings to come. Threads on sale usually have been on the shelf a long time and may be warped and weakened.

Needles and Pins

The best quilting needle is a No. 9 "Between," although some quilters prefer the longer No. 7 and No. 8 "Betweens." The No. 9 is shorter than a regular needle, in order to let you keep your thimbled finger (normally the middle one) behind the end and push it through the fabric comfortably; its large eye is easy to thread.

For holding the layers of material together, use silk pins, which are finer than

47. Heavyweight contrasting-colored threads can constitute a major element of a trapunto design.

regular pins. When sewing a very fine fabric such as a silk or satin, pin with slender, sharp needles rather than pins as they will make smaller holes in the delicate material.

Thimble

A thimble should fit your finger snugly, not tightly. Some quilters find that it's helpful to have several thimbles of different sizes, because a change of thimbles can be almost as relaxing as a change of shoes. There are any number of thimbles available in all different materials, from plastic to beautifully handcrafted Mexican silver, and antique thimbles are fun to collect.

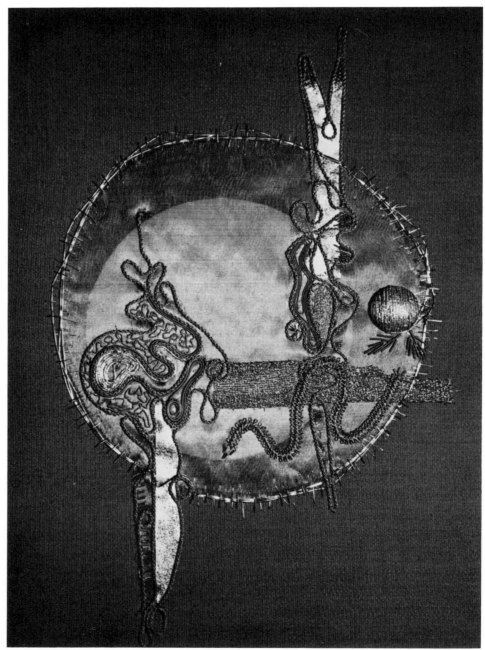

48. "Adam and Eve," wall hanging by Bucky King, shows an interesting use of metallic thread in embroidery stitches. Apple, snake, and other elements are raised by stuffing. (Photo courtesy of the artist)

Scissors

Use a sharp, clean pair of scissors for cutting materials; and try not to use them for anything else. Most of you have been told this; but in case you haven't heard, cutting paper, hair, and so on quickly dulls scissors, making them absolutely no good for cutting material smoothly.

A small pair of embroidery scissors with sharp points is best for opening the backing fabric and cutting thread. They should be sharp enough to cut the thread cleanly, which makes threading your needle much easier.

Before you buy a pair of scissors, try them on for size and weight; comfortable fit in scissors is as important as it is in clothing.

Miscellany

Even when you're not making designs, pencils and a hand ruler or hem gauge should be kept handy for odd jobs like adding a parallel line to a design for cording. Hard lead pencils are usually recommended for needlework; but the lines are so faint that you have to be careful not to lose your sewing guide while stitching. A sharp No. 2 medium-lead pencil makes a slightly darker, longer-lasting mark.

FRAMES

Ask traditional quilters whether you need a frame to do raised quilting, and they are likely to answer, "Absolutely!" A contemporary quilter might disagree, particularly if she or he is working on a small piece such as an article of clothing, a pillow, or a wall hanging. Since quilting was developed well before the frame was invented, it does seem doubtful to claim that it's an *absolute* necessity, but it can be helpful. Quilting with a frame and quilting without one each has its advantages and disadvantages. Whether you use one or not is more a matter of personal choice than anything else.

Quilting without a Frame

Any piece of trapunto work, unless it is unusually large, can be done without a frame, and some quilters feel that even pieces as large as 3 x 5 feet can be handled easily without one. A good rule of thumb is: if the piece wrinkles as you gather it up in your hand to sew, or if it's too large and clumsy to hold comfortably, use a frame.

The big advantage in frameless quilting, of course, is portability. Most quilting frames are too large and awkward to be carried around from place to place, especially public places. Maybe they were fine for quilting bees, which gave women a reason to get together in one place to exchange recipes and information, but for the modern person who likes to work alone and travels often, it's inflexible. Without a frame you can roll up the work and take it along anywhere—in a car, train, bus, or plane; to a friend's house, a doctor's office, or a boxing match, for that matter. If wrinkling is a problem, roll one end of the piece around a cardboard tube instead of gathering it up in your hand.

Quilting without a frame not only makes the work portable, but also somewhat easier to handle when you are sewing (except in the case of a very large piece); and it requires so little room. It's possible that the big, bulky wooden frames used in early quilting were one of the reasons for the decline in the art of making quilted coverlets.

49. **Quilting frame courtesy of Sears, Roebuck & Co.**

Quilting with a Frame

If you prefer to do your needlework at home, or if you have two projects going—one portable and the other static—a frame certainly has significant advantages. The purpose of a frame is to keep the layers of material in place and evenly stretched while you are sewing. Using a frame will ensure a smoother finished piece because there is less chance of puckering the work by pulling threads too tight. While the fabric is stretched on the frame, the relief effect of the trapunto will not be as evident, but once it is released from the frame, the hills and valleys will appear.

There are a number of good commercial quilting frames available at needlecraft shops and departments, larger sewing suppliers, and some hardware stores. Frames like the one in photo 49 can also be ordered through various catalogues (see the list of suppliers for some sources). In addition to the standard adjustable rectangular frames, a quilting hoop is quite suitable for trapunto. This is similar to the two-ring embroidery hoop, except that it is much larger (about 22 inches in diameter) and some of them come with floor stands and adjustable pitch.

You can use a regular embroidery hoop for small trapunto areas; however, if the hoop is smaller than the piece, it will wrinkle the fabrics and will be hard to fasten over padded areas. If the hoop is larger than the piece you are working on, sew fabric to the edges of the piece and fasten the hoop over that (photo 51).

50. The purpose of a frame is to keep materials stretched taut while quilting. Frame here is homemade (see instructions for "yardstick frame" on page 45).

51. Using an embroidery hoop for small trapunto pieces.

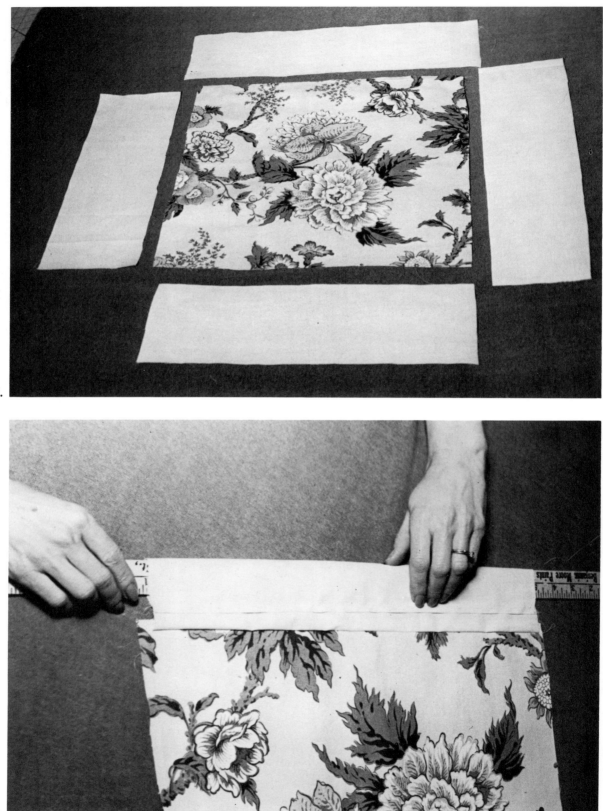

52.

53.

How to Make a Frame

You can also make your own frame. Below are two that you can construct easily with minimal cost:

The "Yardstick Frame"

1. Cut four strips of unbleached muslin (or any sturdy fabric) 5 inches wide, corresponding in length to the four sides of the fabric to be quilted (see photo 52).

2. Stitch a 1½-inch sleeve, lengthwise, in each muslin strip.

3. Machine stitch the (single-thickness) edge of the muslin strips to each of the four edges of your piece, leaving the sleeves outward.

4. Find four pieces of flat wood—such as yardsticks*—less than 1½ inches wide and longer than the edges of your quilting. Slip the sticks into the muslin sleeves (see photo 53).

5. Overlap the sticks at the corners and secure with 1-inch C-clamps (see photo 50).

6. Stretch the top fabric and adjust the clamps until your material is taut. Baste the padding and backing fabrics to the underside of the piece on the frame.

7. Now you can start quilting anywhere, without pinning or basting around the design. You can skip around, quilting a little here, a lot there.

The "Picture Frame"

A second type of quilting frame can be made from an old wooden picture frame or one of the new pre-cut wooden ones that are so easy to assemble. Any sturdy frame will do, but preferably it should be slightly smaller than your piece. If it is the perfect shape and size (lots of luck!) just thumbtack the fabric to the frame, making sure that it is fairly taut. If the frame is larger than your piece, stitch extra fabric to the edges of the piece and thumbtack this to the frame. You can also baste your top fabric (and middle layer of padding, if you are using one) to a permanent backing material that is big enough to fit the frame. Cut off the excess backing when the quilting is complete, or leave it to be sewn around a stiff backing for mounting pictures.

* Slats from the bottom of window shades are fine, but you can usually pick up yardsticks as free advertising handouts from hardware stores or lumberyards.

54. Wall hanging with traditional "Princess Feather" design raised with both cording and stuffing, by Mary Morgan.

Designs

DESIGN SELECTION

This is the good part. Selecting and using the design to the best advantage on a trapunto piece is the real challenge to your creative abilities, and the best advice we can give is to let your imagination go. Although there are certain guidelines that can help you choose a design that is best suited to a particular piece, you should be willing to try anything and to learn from your mistakes and successes.

In choosing the design there are a number of interrelated elements that need to be considered: the weight, texture, and color of the fabric; the shape and size of the design; methods of stitching and raising to be used; the weight and color of the thread; and even the image or "message" the design will convey.

The method of raising has some bearing on the choice, but many designs can be adapted for either basic technique. Even traditional corded and stuffed designs had much in common. The piece in photo 54, for example, shows how one well-known traditional quilting design, the "Princess Feather," can be used for both stuffing and cording. One can generalize by saying that, normally, narrow design areas are more conducive to cording and that wider, more rounded designs are usually better stuffed.

The main things to keep in mind when you are looking for a design to be raised, either by stuffing or cording, are simplicity and clarity. Whether it's already printed on the fabric, or one you must transfer to a solid material, a simple design will display the raised effects better than a complicated one. This is not to say that the design should not have many parts; but each individual part should be sharp-edged, clear, and fairly simple. The tiny floral designs on the pillow in photo 55 and the jungle scene on the block in photo 56 are good examples. Avoid designs with a lot of overlapping in the outline and patterns on pre-designed fabrics that are "fuzzy" or not clearly defined.

Elements of Design and Achieving a Balanced Piece

There are some basic elements of design that can help you achieve a more effective result in your piece. A good design is one that has unity and harmony

47

55. Pre-designed fabric pillow with many tiny, clearly defined design elements. ("Flower Folio" pillow from kit by MM Studios)

56. "Dream," sampler by Sherri Wisoff, of unbleached muslin with polyester batting and fill.

and is in proper scale, or proportion, and balance with the other elements of the piece—fabrics, threads, colors, stitches, and so on. In fact, all of these contribute to the process of designing.

Unity and harmony are extremely important in trapunto. All the components should work together as a whole to present a single, unified, harmonious picture. In other words, the parts should blend in such a way as to present a oneness. This means that the fabrics and the design should agree on the "message" you want to convey; and the color and weight of the thread should be compatible with the texture of the fabric, as well as the size and shape of the design. For instance, if you were to use a silver thread on burlap to outline a delicate, traditional flower there would be little unity in the piece. On the other hand, using a silver thread to outline an elegant geometric design or abstract flower on gray velvet results in harmony. *But don't be afraid to experiment!*

The scale, or size relationship, of the design to the whole is equally important. For example, a small, delicate design can be lost on a large, heavy piece. Thick cording can overpower a dainty design; fine silk thread can underemphasize a heavy, rough cotton fabric or a bold design.

The third element is balance. The design should be arranged in such a way that the visual weight and interest is equal on each half of the piece. This is simple if the design is symmetrical, but when your design is a free one, more care must be taken to achieve the correct visual weight. For example, the airplane on the bottom half of the purse in photo 22 has been balanced by ground quilting lines in the upper part of the piece. To help achieve the proper balance, look at your piece in a mirror—that can give you a fresh perspective on the whole. Also, before you apply the design to the fabrics, draw the overall pattern (outline) of the finished piece on tracing paper and move it around over the design until you find a pleasing placement. (This can be done with both original designs on solid fabrics and pre-designed fabrics.)

Achieving all these elements is a matter of natural progression. An example of one that worked is the chamois pillow in photo 164. The idea grew out of a magazine article on contemporary American Indian pottery, and the design was adapted from one of the pieces shown. Chamois was chosen as a medium because of the importance leather played in the history of the Indian—in home construction, clothing, and furnishing—and because its earthen color is so like the clay used in both old and new Indian crafts. The pure circular shape of the pillow and the uncomplicated three-part design are reminiscent of the simplicity of design and the use of stylized geometric figures in these crafts. Heavy threads of dark earth colors emphasize the designs; and cording, rather than stuffing, was used to raise them because of the boldness and strength the stark raised lines would give to the whole pillow. The designs were arranged within the circle so that no one would dominate the others and so that the heaviest, or largest, would not appear to weigh down one side of the pillow. The fringe wasn't in the original plan; but the edging was not trimmed, leaving an overlapping piece that just naturally suggested the Indian concept of finishing leather items with a decorative fringe.

Designs/Sources

There are almost unlimited sources of designs that will look great in raised quilting. Books are particularly helpful: books about art, archaeology, architecture, history, botany, interior decorating, design, clothing, mythology, even science and mathematics. And what about reference books? A wealth of ideas can be found in a dictionary or encyclopedia, like the butterfly on the velvet skirt in photo 195 which came from a twenty-year-old *Encyclopedia Americana.*

Magazines are even better than books in some ways, mainly because you can cut them up. The design on the chamois pillow in photo 164 was adapted from a magazine photo; the onion in photo 57 came from an art illustration in a periodical.

Art objects and antiques provide many beautiful designs. Paintings, sculpture, pottery, Tiffany lamp shades, stained-glass windows, and Oriental rugs are fairly obvious. The way they are used is not. The yoke and cuffs of the caftan in photo 199 are an adaptation of a simple design copied from a Chinese rug hanging in a shop window.

And, then there's the not-so-obvious—antique buttons, scrolls on the side of a 1930s building, carved wooden doors, grillwork on a potbellied stove, or an ancient tombstone in the neighborhood churchyard. Medallions and coins, like trapunto, are reliefs, and you can see in advance how they will look as raised designs.

You can also commune with nature to get ideas for trapunto designs: trees, flowers, leaves, ferns, stars, animals, humans, and so forth are long-time favorites of all quilters. But look closely at the minute details of natural things for beautiful, unusual ideas; think of the unique shape of a single geranium leaf as the dominant outline on a large pillow, with cording to accent the veins. And don't stop with plant life; take a hint from the thumbprint pillow in photo 156.

Human and animal figures are excellent subjects for three-dimensional art, as can be seen in the pillows in photos 59 and 157.

Home may be where the heart is, but it's also a dandy place to find trapunto designs. In the kitchen, trace around a cookie cutter, copy your china or pottery pattern, sketch a ripe tomato, or borrow a picture from your box of oatmeal. You'll find the work of some of the most talented designers in the country right on your pantry shelf in the form of stylized lettering and well-known product logos—like the little salt girl. You'll find other highly creative commercial designs in advertising flyers, on the side of trucks, on billboards, and in newspapers and magazines.

Trace a design from your favorite carpet or wallpaper; wallpaper sample books are a gold mine, too, for you can trace many designs right out of them already the proper size.

Copy children's coloring and comic books, or their own simple drawings. Or create your own designs. Draw your child's profile—some suggestions for doing life-size profiles are given on page 140—and put it on a pillow, like the one in photo 158. Or trace around his or her little foot or hand. A unique memento for the future would be a record of early foot and hand growth done each year in quilted relief. Make simple sketches of your cat—the one on the pillow in photo 157 is old "Bess" in her favorite pose—a fish, a favorite plant, your golf clubs or tennis racket.

Even if you really can't draw, use your imagination to create original designs. The grape cluster in photo 61 was made by drawing around different-sized coins, starting with nickels at the top of the clump, where the grapes would be more mature, and ending with dimes at the bottom. Many quilt designs are created simply by tracing a cup or glass or by cutting symmetrical patterns from folded paper. Of course, old quilts and books of quilt patterns are one of the best sources of all.

Finding the Right Design on a Pre-Designed Fabric

Most pre-designed fabrics have one dominant pattern motif that will give you an easy choice for a design. Some, like the fabric used on the Persian wall hanging

57. LEFT: Trapunto design of a "ramp onion" from *Pace* magazine. Original design by Nancy R. Gibbs.

58. ABOVE: Eagle adapted from American quarter. Designed and worked by Mary Morgan.

59. BELOW: Pillow by Marcia Shapiro, figures adapted from an art sketch book.

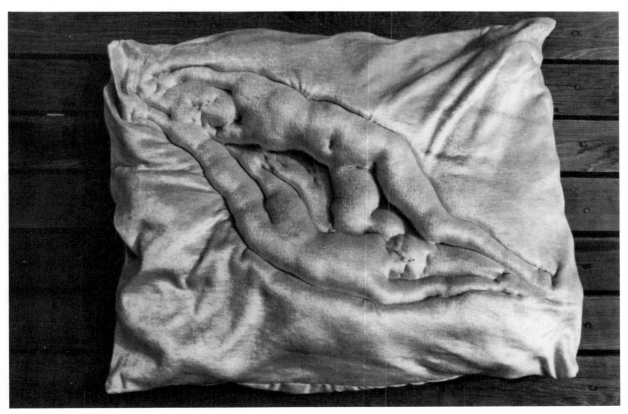

60. BELOW LEFT: Child's pieced blanket, done by Marilla Arguelles, has stuffed animal figures originally drawn by Max Arguelles, the artist's son (shown here with the blanket). Blanket owned by Chris Parker.

61. RIGHT: An original design created by Mary Morgan using coins for templates. Worked on cotton velveteen with gold metallic thread in a running stitch. Grapes stuffed individually.

62. BELOW RIGHT: The design chosen for corded quilting was this heart shape, made into a pillow following the design's own natural lines. Worked by Mary Morgan.

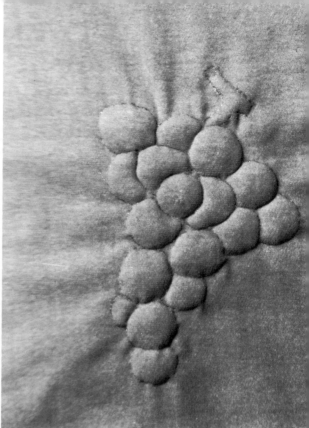

in photo 187, for example, have very definite design groupings which are naturals for a pillow or wall hanging.

Other fabrics, like the rope design on linen in photo 62, are not so obvious. For a fabric like this, it takes a bit of studying to find the best design for raised quilting. The trick is to focus your eye on different areas, squint, walk away, turn it upside down and sideways, and study until you "get it."

On fabrics with an all-over design with no dominant motifs, you can find the best pattern placement a little more scientifically. Use a window template (the outside of a cutout pattern) to position the design.

1. Cut a template the size of the finished piece from a newspaper, cardboard, etc. (This is the pattern for the tea cozy in photo 220.) Take the window portion and place it over the fabric, moving it around until you find the "right" area. (You see exactly what you will get in the finished piece.)

2. Put the solid part back in the window, remove the window, and draw around the template, adding a seam allowance.

63.

64.

The Tools

Pencils: No. 2 lead pencil—for transferring designs to backing, or to top fabric when back stitch or chain stitch is used.

No. 4 lead pencil—makes a fainter line than a No. 2 pencil; can be used on top fabric when running stitch is done.

White dressmakers' pencil—for drawing designs on dark fabrics; available at most sewing supply outlets.

Felt tip pens: India ink pens—produce dark, solid lines; should be used on backing fabric only, and never when top fabric is light enough for lines to show through.

Easier to use than pencils for they will not pull the fabrics as you draw. India ink-type pens only are waterfast. (Very important, for a drop of tea or a teardrop will not cause them to run!) Available in art supply stores.

Regular felt tips pens—for drawing patterns on paper or cardboard, but not fabric, as they are not waterfast.

Paper: Tracing paper—for design transfer and layout (invaluable).

Lightweight paper—for cutting folded paper patterns.

Heavyweight paper—for cutting templates and other patterns that do not have to be folded.

Newsprint: A roll of newsprint, or yesterday's newspaper, is a most economical pattern-making tool.

Tailor's chalk: For tracing patterns on top fabric—particularly useful when a running stitch is used as it will wash or brush off after the sewing is complete. Be careful, as it will also disappear easily with handling.

Ruler/yardstick: For many uses in design making and application.

Iron-on transfer designs: For transferring designs from paper to fabrics; available through quilting supply outlets (some sources are in the list of suppliers).

Iron-on transfer pencils: Excellent for drawing designs on tracing paper to be transferred by iron to fabrics. Lines can be washed out of most natural fabrics

65. Using a stencil to transfer designs. (Stencil from Needleart Guild)

with soap and water, but not most blends or synthetics. (Test any fabric before you apply the design.)

Carbon paper: Special dressmakers' carbon paper for applying designs to fabric is available in most sewing outlets. Designs can be drawn directly onto fabric with tracing wheel, ballpoint pen, or sharpened pencil. (*Do not use typing carbon!*)

Tracing wheel: A small serrated wheel that can be used to apply a design with dressmaker carbon paper. Available in most sewing supply outlets; also comes in kits with carbon paper and instructions in many of the larger outlets.

Templates: A simple tool used by needlecrafters and engineers alike to make designs, it is a master pattern usually cut from some fairly rigid material (stiff paper, cardboard, sandpaper, etc.). There are two types of templates: solid (photo 64), and window (photo 63), which has the middle cut out or made transparent so you can place it over the fabric to determine the best location for cutting out or drawing the design. Commercial templates, made primarily for patchwork, are available from a number of quilting design sources in various shapes and sizes (sources may be found in the list of suppliers).

Cardboard: For making templates and stiff backing used in mounting wall hangings. (Save the backing from shirts that have been sent to the laundry.)

Stencils: Special quilting pattern stencils are available from many sources (some are included in the list of suppliers). Lettering and geometric pattern stencils are also available in art supply shops and department and hardware stores.

Grid paper: A paper marked in squares, used in enlarging and reducing designs (see page 65) and for tracing embossed items, such as coins, for subsequent enlargement.

Applying the Design

There are many ways to apply a design; whether you transfer it to the top or the backing fabric will be determined by the method of stitching you want to use.

Designs are most often transferred to the backing, but in that case, you are limited to using a running stitch for quilting. Two important things to remember when transferring designs to the backing are: (1) the design on the backing will be reversed on the top; so, numbers and monograms, or any other design that is not symmetrical on both sides, must be reversed when transferred to backing; and (2) dark lines on the backing may show through light-colored top fabrics.

Any stitch may be used when the design is applied to the top fabric, but light, thin transfer lines should be made so that the stitches will cover them. It is best to use a hard-lead pencil if a running stitch is to be used as tracing lines will show between the stitches (pencil marks will disappear with erasing or the first laundering). It's not necessary to remove pencil lines for show. You will often see quilts on exhibit with light pencil lines still visible.

Tracing

The easiest and most commonly used method of applying a design is by tracing it directly onto the fabric. Place the design on a smooth background—a light-colored surface, such as a white counter top or washing machine, will make things easier. Set the fabric over the design and move it around until you find the proper placement. Secure it with pins or tape to keep the work from shifting as you trace. Hold the fabric down with your free hand as you trace so that you can see through the material better and so that the pencil point will not pull and move the fabric.

If the piece is small enough to handle easily, you can hold it up to a window pane and let the natural light show through. Of course, tracing over a light box is the easiest way of all.

Using Carbon Paper to Transfer Designs

This method can be used on either the top fabric or the backing; however, if done on top, a solid line of stitches should be made to cover the lines, for they will not always come out in the wash.

1. Place the carbon paper face down on the fabric, with the design on top of that. Pin or tape fabric, carbon, and design together so they will not shift in the transfer.

2. Using a tailor's wheel, ballpoint pen, or sharp, hard-lead pencil, trace around the design, exerting enough pressure to make a clearly visible line on the fabric.

Iron-On Transfers

There are lovely commercial iron-on patterns available, especially in England, which you can simply iron off the paper onto the fabric. But you can also make your own with an iron-on transfer pencil.

1. To make a permanent pattern that can be transferred to either top or backing, trace the design onto tracing paper with an iron-on transfer pencil. This will be a master pattern, and when you need to reapply it (after two or three iron-ons), simply go over all the lines again with the iron-on pencil.

2. With iron-on transfers, the design must be reversed if it is to be put on the top fabric or it will appear backwards in the finished piece. If the design goes on the backing, the transfer should not be reversed. (The eagle on the wall hanging in photo 58 was a goof with an iron-on transfer. Its head points in the opposite direction from its counterpart on the quarter, because the design was reversed on the backing fabric. There is also a left-handed hot mitt in the "oops" box because of the same type of mistake!)

3. Keep a sharp point on your transfer pencil or the lines will be too thick. The design on the tea cozy in photo 222 was made from a pattern oulined with a dull transfer pencil; consequently, the lines are wider than the solid stitching lines, so that they show (and they did not come out of the synthetic fabric, even with scrubbing).

4. Test the fabrics to see if the transfer lines will come out with laundering. Synthetics and blends seem to retain these transfer pencil lines.

5. To transfer, place the design face down on the fabric and press, following the instructions that come with the pencil. To check, lift the edge of the transfer carefully, so as not to move the paper. If you are not able to get it back down in exactly the same position, you'll end up with a double outline.

Using Templates and Stencils

Another way to trace a design directly onto a fabric is by using a template pattern or stencil (photo 65). Templates are particularly handy, especially when the design is composed of one or more very simple figures like the Indian pattern on the chamois pillow in photo 164. Templates can also be used as patterns for the general outline of the piece.

1. Draw the design on stiff paper or cardboard. You can do this by putting the original design on top of carbon paper over the cardboard and tracing it onto the cardboard, or by cutting the design out of tracing paper first and drawing around it on the stiff paper.

2. Cut out the templates and arrange them on the fabric, moving them around until you get the proper results. (This way you can see what you're getting, and make adjustments, before you draw on the fabric.) Hold the template in place and trace around it.

66.

Pricking and Pouncing

This is an old-fashioned method of transferring a design, but it's still very effective. A punched pattern will last and last.

1. Punch (prick) holes in the design (on paper) with a pin or a sewing machine set on a long stitch and without thread. Commercial patterns with the holes already punched are also available. Before pouncing, take a piece of fine sandpaper and smooth off the rough edges of the holes so that the pattern will lie flat against the materials.

2. A tablespoon of cornstarch, tied up in a little square of backing fabric, makes a good pouncer for dark fabrics. For light fabrics, grind up colored chalk.

3. Pat (pounce) and rub the pouncer over the holes so that the powder goes through to the fabric, creating dotted lines. Take a peek at the beginning to see that the powder is going through the holes, but be careful not to move the pattern or you may end up with double lines.

67.

4. Remove the pattern and connect the dots, using a lead pencil for light fabrics and a white dressmakers' pencil for darker ones. Shake or brush the fabric to remove the powder.

68.

Caftan. See pages 172–77.

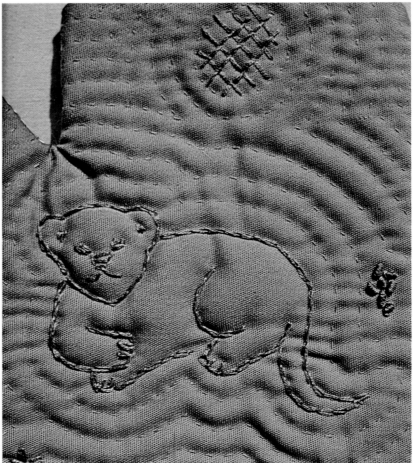

Palm of hot mitt. See page 204.

Back of hot mitt. See page 204.

Pincushion. See page 194.

Pet pillow. See page 139.

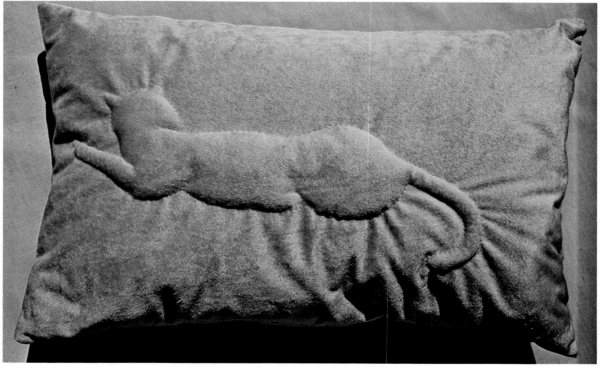

Clown face quilt block. See pages 110–17.

Chamois pillow. See page 144.

Green thumb pillow. See page 138.

Sampler block. See page 69.

Christmas tree.
See pages 154–55.

Square tea cozy.
See pages 194–95.

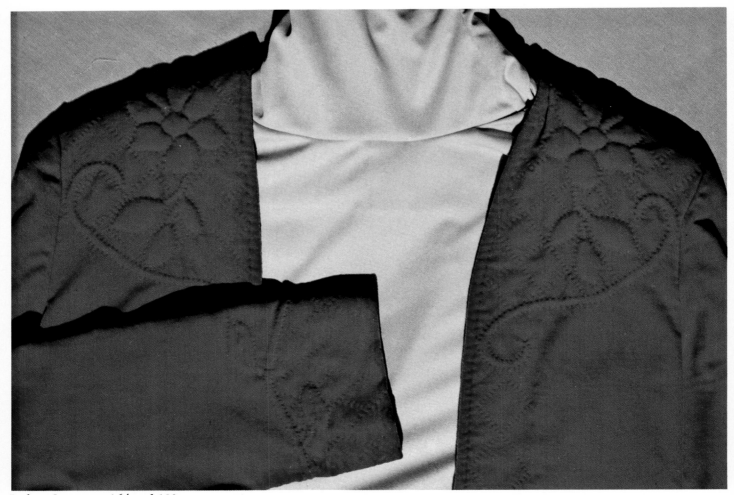

Jacket. See pages 164 and 183.

69. Angel wall hanging was made from a rubbing of the top part of an 1800s tombstone, by Mary Morgan.

Making Designs from Rubbings

Quilters have found that the relief designs on tombstones in old churchyards offer interesting artwork for trapunto. The wall hanging in photo 69 was done from the top design of a stone; but if the epitaph is plain enough, it, too, can be quilted and become part of the raised design. Elsa Brown's wall hanging in photo 71 was made from a rubbing of an entire tombstone.

Rubbings are made by placing newsprint or an old newspaper on top of the area you wish to raise, rubbing across it with the side of a peeled wax crayon (photo 70). The design can then be traced and transferred onto the fabric.

Designs can also be taken from coins and other small embossed items in the same basic way: by covering the object with paper and rubbing over its surface with the side of a pencil lead.

70.

71. "Life Is Uncertain," wall hanging from tombstone rubbing by Elsa Brown. Made of polyester/nylon semi-sheer fabric, machine stitched. The wall hanging includes the epitaph from the stone. (Photo courtesy of the artist)

Cutting Folded Paper Designs

Many years ago, it was a pastime and an artistic endeavor of young ladies to cut pictures and designs from folded paper, mount them on dark backgrounds, and frame them. This was, perhaps, the origin of the Hawaiian quilt symmetrical pattern appliqués. Traditional quilters also used this elementary technique, which we all learned in the third grade, to create highly original designs. Often a square with multiple designs was used as a master pattern for each of the blocks in a quilt. In case you've forgotten how, here are some suggestions for making designs and patterns from paper. You'll be surprised at how much fun it still is.

Start with a square piece of paper. Fold it in half, diagonally or straight across. Fold it again, and again. You can go as far as you like, or as far as you can go and still get the scissors to cut through all the layers. The more you fold, of course, the more times each design will appear. For example, if you cut a design after only one fold, you'll get only one design. Cut it after the second fold and you get two. After the third fold, you get four; after the fourth fold, eight . . . and so on, the number doubling each time you fold the paper.

You can vary a design by cutting at different folds. The design in photos 72 and 73, for example, was done by cutting the horizontal pattern on the first fold and the vertical pattern on the second. Another way to change the appearance is to fold the paper once or twice, cut designs on both edges; fold again, move the scissors up the edge and cut a design on each edge; and so forth.

The designs you can make this way are literally endless. Each one seems fresh and exciting, for, indeed, there never was another like it in the world.

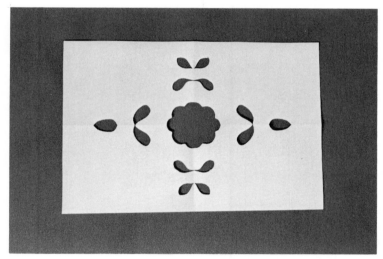

72. Cut-paper design.

73. Gray silk sampler made from cut-paper design in photo 72.

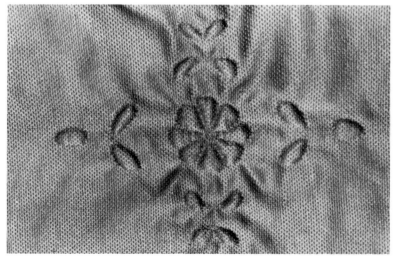

Making a Five-Point "Star-Fold"

You probably learned this one at the slightly advanced age of a fourth grader —and promptly forgot it. It isn't easy to remember, and it isn't really very easy to do, because it involves some fairly complex folding and measuring. A five-point star-fold was used to make the pincushion in photo 218.

These instructions for making a five-point star-fold will produce a pattern 6 inches in diameter, a proper size for a pincushion. Measurements are also given for cutting 10- and 12-inch patterns, suitable for quilt blocks and pillows.

1. Cut a 6-inch square of paper. Fold in half diagonally (1st fold). See fig. 1.
2. Measure center of 1st fold and mark A. From bottom corner (B), measure 2½ inches* along bottom edge and mark C. Fold top down to meet C (2nd fold). See fig. 2.
3. Fold down on 3rd fold line, bringing D to match C.
4. Fold back on 4th fold line, bringing B behind to edge of 3rd fold line.
5. Cut the pattern. (Fig. 5 is the pattern for the pincushion in photo 218.)

* For a 10-inch star-fold, the measurement from B to C is 4½ inches; for a 12-inch star-fold, it is 5 inches.

Working with Half- and Quarter-Patterns

Any design that is symmetrical—that is, with both halves, or all four quarters, the same—can be made from a half- or quarter-pattern. Some of the designs in this book have been halved or quartered so that they will not have to be enlarged when you transfer them to a fabric. The following are instructions for using a half-pattern.

1. Start with tracing paper that is twice as large as the design. (You need room to add the other half later.) Fold it in half and make a crease down the center. Open it and line up the crease with the center line of the design. Trace the design. (Use iron-on transfer pencil for one-step application.) See photos 74 and 75.
2. Refold the paper, leaving the tracing on the outside. Place this tracing face down on the drawing table (a white surface helps) and trace it onto the other half of the paper. When you unfold the sheet, you'll have a whole design, with both halves drawn on the same side of the paper. (That is absolutely necessary for ironing on designs, of course.)
3. For a design like the eagle in these pictures, add the head to one side only. On the second half of the body, omit the line for the neck. After opening up the sheet, match the dotted lines of the pattern with the proper place on the tracing, and add the head.

For a quarter-pattern, simply fold the paper in quarters, crease, and unfold. Trace the design first on one section, and then on each of the other three sections, from the original in sequence so that the design meets at the folds.

Designs 62

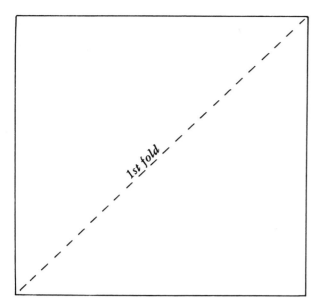

Fig. 1.

Fig. 2.

B   2½″   C

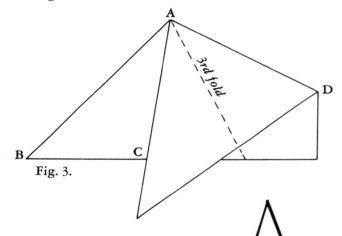

Fig. 3.

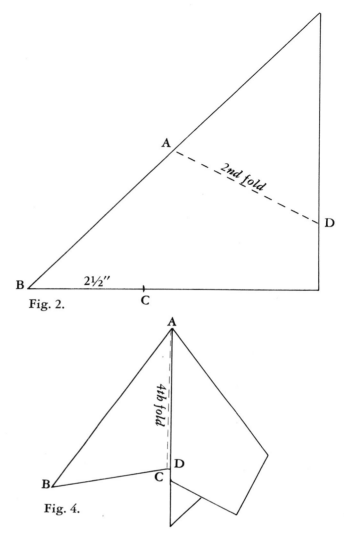

Fig. 4.

Fig. 5. Five-fold cutting
pattern for pincushion in
photo 218 (6-inch
diameter).

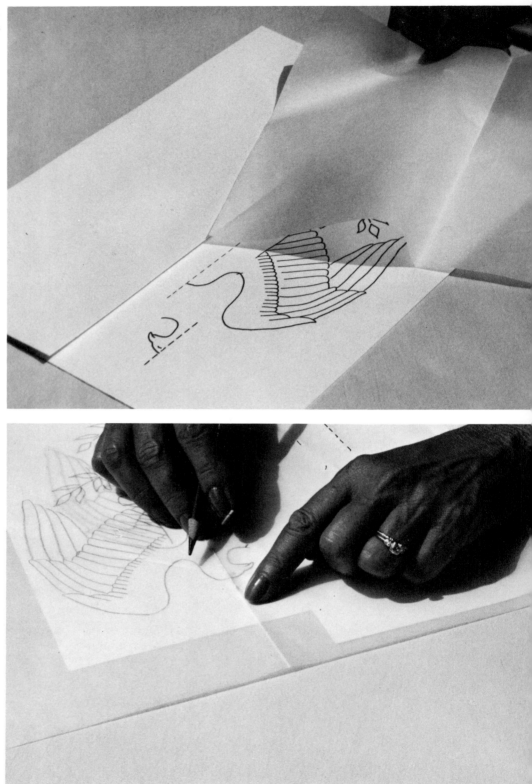

74. Step 1 of tracing a half-pattern. See page 62.

75. Adding the non-symmetrical portion of a half-pattern. See page 62.

Enlarging and Reducing Designs

You will often find a design you want to use that is not the right size in its original form; but no design is too large or too small, because just about anything can be reduced or enlarged in some way.

The easiest way is to take the design to any commercial photostat establishment and have it quickly blown up or reduced for a few dollars. But there are mechanical methods for changing the size of a design which you can use yourself. One is an inexpensive commercial reproduction device called a pantograph, available in art supply stores and craft shops.

There are also projectors (called vugraphs) that will pick up a picture from any source and project it any size you want. You can buy one—though the good ones are fairly expensive—in a large art supply store; or you can probably find one in a local school, Scout hut, or other educational-type facility.

Enlarging and reducing can also be done by the grid method, with a little patience and minimal equipment.

1. Trace the design from the original source onto a piece of tracing paper. Divide the paper, over the design, into equal-size squares by drawing vertical and horizontal lines, making sure that the design is completely covered by the squares. This is called a grid. (You can also use commercially printed grid paper to trace from the original to avoid having to make your own grid.) The best size square is ¼ inch if you are enlarging, and ½ or 1 inch if you are reducing (see photo 76).

2. Letter the squares across the top and number them going down.

76.

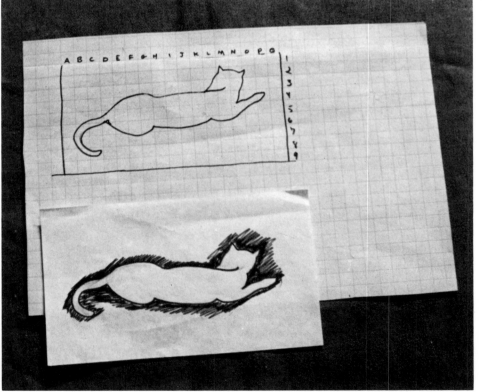

77.

3. On a second piece of paper, sketch in the general outline of the design the size you want it to be. (It will be easier if you enlarge or reduce the size of the original by an even number, that is, to make it twice as large, or three times as large, rather than two-and-a-half times as large; or, if reducing, half or one-fourth as large, etc.) Divide the paper into a grid with the same number of squares as are in the original grid. (They will be twice, three times, etc., as large, or one-fourth, etc., as large.) Letter them across the top and number going down, so that they correspond to the letters and numbers in the original.

4. Copy the design from the original squares to the corresponding squares in the new grid one square at a time.

Changing the Shape of a Design

If you want to make a design longer, use the grid method for enlarging, only make the squares to which you are transferring your design longer than those on the original. To make a design shorter, make the transfer squares shorter; to make it wider or narrower, make the transfer squares wider or narrower.

USING TRADITIONAL DESIGNS

From traditional quilting we can find, and adapt, many beautiful designs for raised work. As mentioned before, old quilts and books of old quilt designs are a rich source of ideas for modern quilters. Look at the details in the oldest surviving quilt, the "Sicilian Quilt," for example, in photos 5 and 6. This is a true portfolio of animal, human, and botanical figures.

78. Early eighteenth-century English coverlet affords many design motifs for modern trapunto, including corded shell pattern, rope twist, and feather design. Made of linen, quilted with linen thread in back stitch.

79. This late nineteenth-century American pieced quilt is a fine source of modern trapunto designs. Two of the raised designs from this quilt were copied in the contemporary samplers in photos 44 and 45 as was the design on the baby's cap in photo 206. (From the Hock Collection, photo by Myron Miller)

In traditional quilting, the designs were classically rigid and almost always used in repetitive patterns. Traditional designs fell into three categories: border designs, background or fill patterns, and central design motifs. In contemporary trapunto, however, you are allowed a great deal of flexibility, and repetition is not used all that often. Designs can be taken from old quilts and used as they are in different settings; ground quilting and border patterns can be adapted as central motifs; traditional figures such as flowers and leaves can be stylized; and so on. The variations of traditional designs and techniques that can be used make this a very creative venture.

Here's how you can make and use some of the favorites among the great old designs.

Hexagons

From pieced quilting, borrow a hexagonal (six-sided) template (photo 80) to create what is known as a "tumbling block" design. The template is used in three different placements, as is shown in fig. 6, to make a design with blocklike perspective. For the piece in photo 80, a ¼-inch channel for cording was added to the edges of the template, and different-colored threads were used to quilt each side of the block to add more of a feeling of three dimensions. (In patchwork this perspective is achieved by using dark and light fabrics in the same arrangement.) Other templates (and shapes) used for pieced work can be adapted for stuffing and cording in this same way. Designs like the hexagon also can be arranged to form a border on clothing or other articles, or to frame another design. For example, a diamond template was used as a ground quilted border for the front lapels of the velveteen jacket in photo 205.

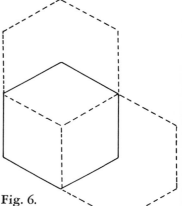

Fig. 6.

Tumbling block pattern. Make template (from solid-line hexagon) of cardboard. Trace template onto paper in solid-line position. Move template to positions indicated by dotted lines and trace to achieve tumbling block perspective.

80. Tumbling block design, created by using hexagonal template borrowed from patchwork quilting, is done on white Oxford cloth with different-colored embroidery threads to achieve depth perception. Worked by Mary Morgan.

Diamonds

Also known as the lozenge pattern in traditional quilting, the diamond shape has been used in every type of quilting, from flat to raised, usually as ground quilting. You can see it in traditional work in photos 8 and 17; and in modern needlecraft as a central design motif on the halter top in photo 81. (The use of the diamond as background quilting for trapunto is discussed on page 87.)

To make an overall diamond pattern, start with a set of parallel lines drawn with a ruler as a guide. Then draw a second set of parallel lines that cross the first lines at an angle. You can make the diamond "fatter" or "thinner" by moving the ruler to different angles.

The diamond pattern can be turned into the traditional "diaper" (three-sided) design by drawing another set of lines that cut the diamonds in half, creating two adjoining triangles within each diamond.

81. Halter top, with corded shell and diamond design motifs, by Mary Morgan.

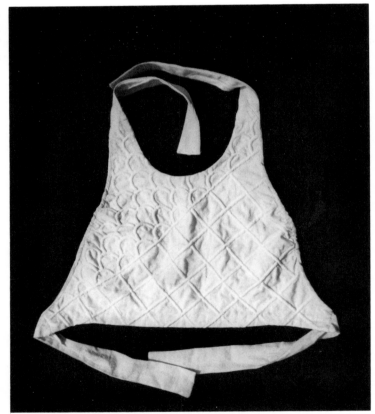

The Shell, or Teacup, Pattern

This may look a little complicated, but it is really just a series of semicircles drawn by tracing around a teacup or other circular item. The shell was used as both ground quilting and an overall motif, as in the coverlet in photo 78, in traditional quilting. A modern adaptation is the overall motif of the corded shell in the halter top in photo 81.

To make a shell:

1. Mark the center lines on the edge of a cup.

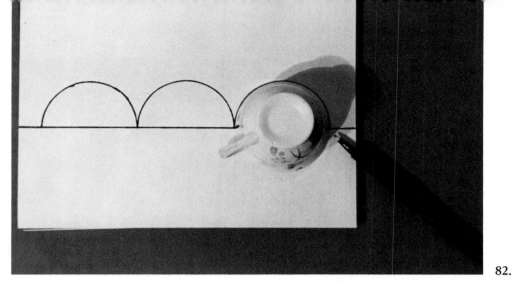

82.

2. Place the cup face down on a piece of paper so that the center marks correspond with a line drawn on the paper. Draw a half-circle around the cup, stopping at the line on each end. Move the cup to the right, where it is just touching the first circle, and draw a second half-circle, and so on, until you have a row of half-circles. (You can vary the design, as was done on the halter, by leaving a space between the edges of the circles.)

83.

3. For the next row up, place the cup so that the bottom of the rim touches the spot where two half-circles on the row below meet. The center marks of the cup should touch the tops of the two circles on either side.

4. Continue in this manner, moving up and outlining until you have enough shells to cover the entire area. (If you use an iron-on transfer pencil, the pattern will be ready for transfer when you finish outlining.)

5. To form a channel for cording, draw a parallel line ¼ inch inside each half-circle, either by measuring and marking dots ¼ inch from the original half-circles and connecting the dots, or by using a compass or smaller cup.

84. Unending rope design
on chair seat.

Unending Border Patterns

Many of the basic quilting border designs can be adapted for use in raised quilting, as either a border or central design motif. To make an unending border which turns corners and/or doubles back to meet itself, follow this technique, which was used to "construct" the rope design on the chair seat in photo 84.

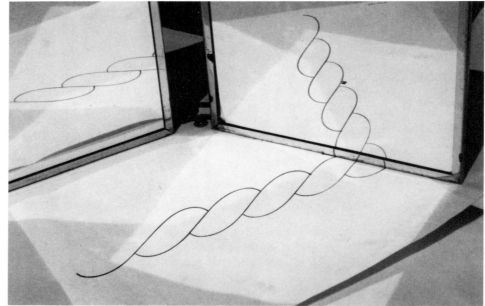

85.

1. On two separate pieces of tracing paper, make a 4- to 5-inch section of the design. (The second one should be reversed.) Place one of the tracings under a mirror, and turn the mirror until you can see the proper angle for a corner that

will fit your design area. Mark the design where the edge of the mirror touches it. On the reverse design, trace that same mark in the proper spot. (This will be the center of the corner section.)

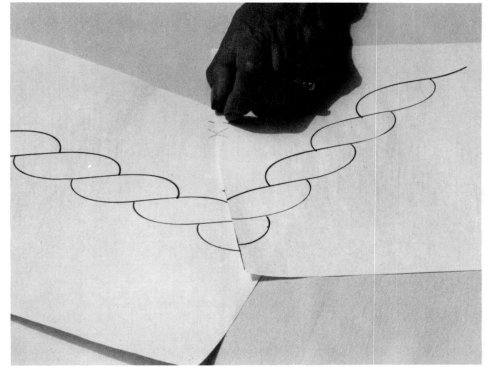

86.

2. Place the two sections one on top of the other, and match the corner marks. Tape them together, take a third piece of tracing paper, and trace the completed design (of two sides and a corner) from the original two pieces.

3. To make an unending rope pattern, trace all four corners the same way.

Many unique designs can be developed from a simple pattern using this technique.

Quilting

STITCHES

The stitches in regular quilting serve two purposes: they hold the layers of fabric together, and they outline the design. Trapunto stitches have still another use: they hold in place the extra padding which creates the raised areas unique to this type of quilting. In some cases the stitches, or the threads used in the stitching, also constitute a major element of the design.

Like the craft itself, the basic stitches are quite easy; to do them well, however, takes a little practice. You can also increase the challenge of the quilting by choosing a slightly more complicated decorative stitch. There are a number that you can use, but the five hand stitches and the techniques for machine stitching discussed in this chapter should cover almost any type of raised quilting you want to do.

The stitches most commonly used in raised quilting are the *running stitch* and the *back stitch*. Both are used for outlining designs, and in ground quilting the running stitch is used predominantly. The running stitch is easier to do; it is also the stitch that can be used when the design is transferred to the backing. The back stitch creates a stronger outline and must be done from the top.

Where the padding in the raised area is too thick to use a running or back stitch, you have two options: the simpler *stab stitch* (used for outlining by many quilters who work on a frame) and the *semi-back stitch*. Both are done from the top and result in an appearance similar to a running stitch.

To add a more decorative quality to the work, several embroidery stitches can be used to quilt. The *chain stitch* is the one used most often in the projects in this book. It is relatively easy to do yet it creates a beautiful and unique effect, particularly when done with metallic thread, as in the velvet sampler in photo 107 or thread that contrasts with the fabric.

There are even occasions when you may wish to use a machine stitch to save time on long, straight lines, such as the parallel lines for Italian quilting.

The following general instructions and tips for stitching are based on the experience (and pierced fingers) of many quilters and are passed on to you as hard-won guides to fast, comfortable, beautiful stitching. As you continue to sew, you'll develop a rhythm and perhaps even your own techniques; you will also discover that your stitches reflect your moods and attitudes. (As a matter of fact, it might be more interesting to read stitches than handwriting to determine a person's character!)

General Guidelines for Quilting Stitches

There are a few things to keep in mind for all types of stitching in raised quilting:

1. Use a single thread, no more than a yard long, as a longer thread will wear out from being pulled through the material too many times, or tend to knot. In the case of heavier threads and metallic threads, an even shorter length is better. You can measure a yard by holding the spool up to your nose and stretching the loose end of the thread as far as your other arm will extend.

2. Cut the thread on an angle; it's easier to thread a needle when the thread comes to a point. And you can prevent snarls by threading the end cut nearest the spool through the needle first.

3. Before you start the actual project, practice on a piece of the same fabric. Quilting is like dancing; it helps to limber up and develop a rhythm each time you begin. No matter how many years a quilter has been sewing, the first stitches of the day are seldom the same as those that follow. Some perfectionists pull out their first few inches of stitching and start over every time just on general principle. It's also a good idea to get a feel for the materials you'll be sewing on, especially if you have added a middle layer of batting.

4. It's important always to quilt through all layers of material, because the stitches are the only thing that hold the layers together and the filler material in place.

5. Make your stitches small, uniform in length and in spacing. The length of a quilting stitch will be determined by the weight and texture of the fabrics you are working with, as well as by personal choice. A good length to start with is about $\frac{1}{8}$ inch; but consistency and uniformity are really more important than length. If you are outlining an irregular shape, the stitches will have to vary somewhat to conform to the pattern.

6. Achieving the proper tension in the thread is another important aspect of quilting. This is particularly critical when a layer of batting is sandwiched between the top and backing fabrics. In that case, the stitches depress the batting, creating the soft rippled effect in the fabric which is one of the lovely things about wadded quilting. A slack thread will not depress it enough; a thread pulled too tight will pucker the fabric. A tight tension can be corrected by stretching the fabric while stitching. (This will not be so much of a problem if the work is stretched on a frame, or when you are sewing on two layers of fabric.)

7. Learn to use a thimble. A lot of you are going to groan at this, but you'll increase your output and comfort 100 percent by using one. With a thimble, you don't have to tug to pull the needle through the fabric, or push with a bare finger. Many professional quilters wear a second thimble on the finger they hold underneath the piece as a protection when the point of the needle comes through the fabric. If you do a great deal of quilting, give this a try.

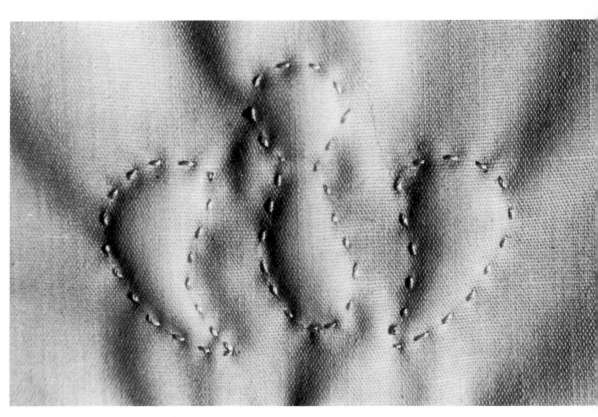

87. **Running stitch.**

The Running Stitch

Just as its name suggests, this stitch is accomplished by running a needle through the fabrics in a single in-out motion; and it can be used whether you are working on two layers of material or three. The simple running stitch has been used universally for all types of quilting for at least as long as our earliest surviving examples.

1. Starting from the underside, bring the needle up at A coming out on the outline you are going to follow. Insert the tip back into the fabric, at B, on the outline, a stitch-length ahead of A. Push it through the materials until you feel the point with your forefinger (fig. 7). (This way you know that the needle has gone through all layers of fabric.)

Fig. 7.

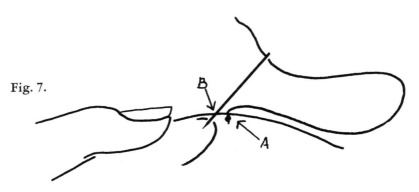

2. Bring the needle back up at C, about a stitch-length ahead of B, and push it all the way through the fabrics (fig. 8). You have completed one running stitch by going in and out in one motion. (When working with thin fabrics and/or stitching straight lines, you will often find that it is possible to pick up more than one stitch at a time on the needle.)

3. A row of running sitches will form a broken outline. The stitches and the spaces between them should all be uniform in length.

Fig. 8.

The Back Stitch

One of the earliest of the traditional quilting techniques, the back stitch, was the mainstay of raised quilting done in the fifteenth through eighteenth centuries in Europe. It is slower to do than the running stitch, but it produces a stronger, more dramatic design element. The back stitch is done on pieces where the design has been drawn on the top fabric; its solid outline will hide the transfer or tracing lines. A heavier thread, such as embroidery floss or buttonhole twist, will produce a better-looking result than a finer thread.

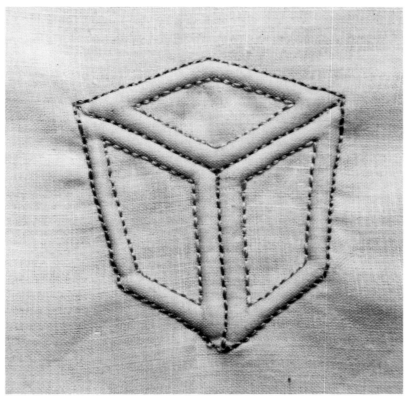

88. Back stitch.

1. Starting from the underside, bring the needle up at A, on the outline, and pull the thread all the way through. Take a small backward stitch, inserting the needle at B, and bring it back up at C, a stitch-length ahead of A. Pull the needle all the way through (fig. 9).

2. Insert the needle at A, right at the end of the last stitch, and bring it back up again a short distance ahead at D (fig. 10).

3. Continue in this manner, so that you produce an unbroken line of even stitches on both the top and the bottom. When you have mastered this stitch, try using a stab stitch technique on an embroidery hoop. Make very small stitches. (This will be more like the stitching done in very early pieces.)

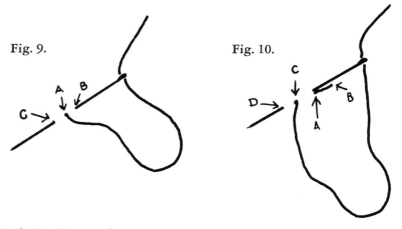

Fig. 9.   Fig. 10.

The Stab Stitch

The stab stitch is an easy, but somewhat time-consuming, quilting technique. In raised quilting, it is generally used when extra fill has been added to raise an area, making it impossible to do a smooth running stitch in/out motion. (This technique is also used in regular quilting, generally when the work is on a hoop or frame.) It is done literally by stabbing the needle into the materials. The depth of the depression it creates will be determined by how tightly the thread is pulled and by how much padding has been added.

1. Starting on the underside, insert the needle straight up at A, coming out on the outline. Pull the thread all the way through. Insert (stab) the needle at B, a running stitch-length ahead of A (fig. 11).

2. Pull the needle all the way through the layers and tighten the thread to depress the padding. (It will help to keep the thread tight and the padding down if you take a small back stitch from time to time on the underneath side.)

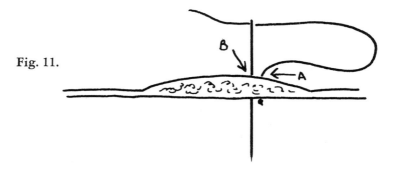

Fig. 11.

The Semi-Back Stitch

Another stitch that is effective in depressing areas that already have been raised is the semi-back stitch. It is used to depress padded areas only slightly and, therefore, it is not necessary to take it all the way through the padding and backing as you do with the stab stitch. This stitch produces a broken-line effect similar to that of the stab and running stitches.

1. Starting on the underside, bring the needle out at A, on the outline. Insert it at B, one stitch-length behind A. Dip the needle into the padding, without catching the backing material, and bring it up at C, two stitch-lengths ahead of A (fig. 12).

2. Pull the thread all the way through and tighten it to depress the fabrics. Continue in this manner.

Fig. 12.

The Chain Stitch

One of the loveliest embroidery stitches that can be used to outline a design, or simply to add a decorative touch to the design details, is the chain stitch. This stitch would be used when you want the stitching to be a definite part of the design, and embroidery thread or silk buttonhole twist are most effective. The chain stitch must always be worked from the top side of the piece, and its thickness will cover fine, light transfer lines on the fabric.

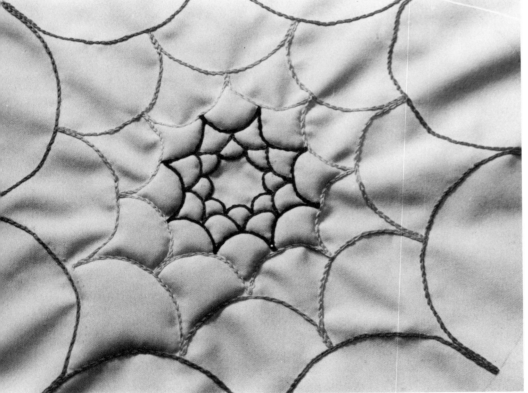

89. Chain stitch.

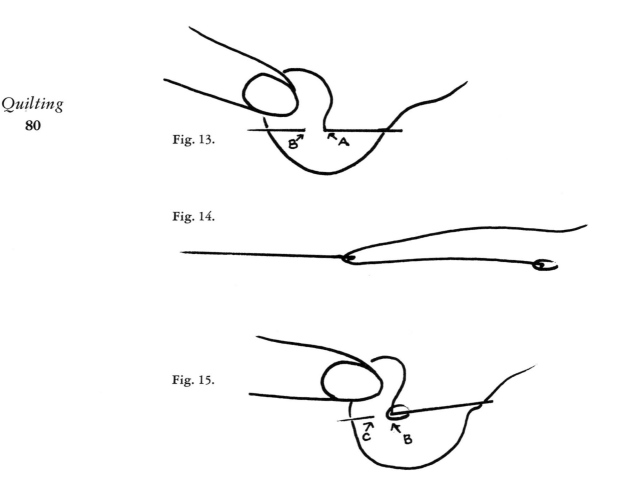

Fig. 13.

Fig. 14.

Fig. 15.

It's wise to do a little extra practicing on this stitch before you apply needle to your good fabrics; and don't be discouraged. It will come to you in one of those little flashes of understanding that one has when something finally sinks in. It's a lovely stitch, and fun to make.

1. Starting on the underside, bring the thread up from the back at A, on the outline. Pull it all the way through. Hold the slack thread under the thumb of your free hand (this forms a sort of loop in the thread). Re-insert the needle at A, in the same hole, and bring it up at B, a stitch-length ahead (fig. 13). Pull the needle and thread to the left, making sure that you come through the loop formed by holding the thread with your thumb.

2. As you pull the thread, the loop will tighten around the thread that is coming out of the fabric (fig. 14). Always pull to the left. If you pull to the right, the loop will shorten and vanish.

3. You have your first link of the chain. Holding the slack thread under your thumb, insert the needle at B, inside, and at the end, of the last chain loop. Bring the needle out at C, a stitch-length ahead, and pull to the left (fig. 15). (Pulling the thread to the left each time with an even tension will give you an even stitch.)

Variations on the Chain Stitch

If you want to change the appearance of the chain stitch, try one of these variations.

The visual effect can be altered significantly by varying the lengths of the loops in the chain, in a repeated pattern. You can use almost any pattern, as long as it fits the design. (Remember, however, that if these stitches will be holding the extra fill in place, they shouldn't be excessively long.)

To add an accent, lace a contrasting-colored, metallic, or different-weight thread up and down through the loops of a row of chain stitching. The secondary thread should not go through the fabrics at all; rather, it is laced behind the loops. The horizontal lines in the ear of corn on the hot mitt in photo 225 were accented by threading a different-colored thread through the original stitch. Photo 90 shows a number of variations on the chain stitch.

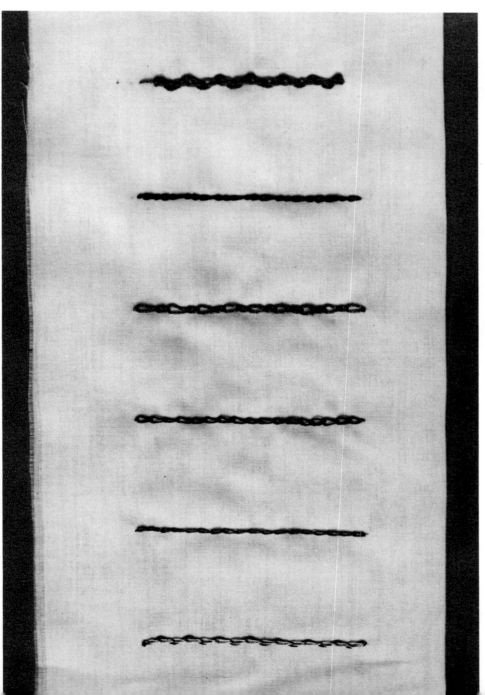

90. Variations on the chain stitch (from top to bottom): blue cotton embroidery floss with red laced up and down between loops and backing fabric—not sewn into fabric; black silk buttonhole twist with repeat pattern of two small loops followed by a longer one; linen embroidery thread with repeat pattern of one short loop, one longer loop; regular chain stitch with button and carpet (heavy) thread; silk buttonhole twist with lacing of fine gold thread between chain stitch and fabric; silk buttonhole twist with lacing of contrasting color in same thread.

91. Machine stitching on
the top fabric.

Machine Stitching

Nothing seems to surpass the sense of accomplishment that comes from doing a piece of needlework entirely by hand, but more and more the sewing machine is becoming a tool of original creativity. Certain designs, particularly those with long, straight lines such as the spiderweb in photo 91, are very well adapted to machine stitching. This is not to say that smaller, more complex designs cannot be done on the machine—the intricate floral patterns in the bridesmaid cap in photo 210 and the figures in the jewelry in photo 92 were machine stitched. But it is sometimes more difficult to stitch a complicated design on the machine than by hand.

Some general guidelines for machine stitching follow:

1. Small, irregular designs are less difficult if your machine has a darning foot which allows you to move the fabric freely as you stitch.

2. It's important to keep the layers of fabric from shifting as you work; so baste them securely together before you start.

3. Don't reverse stitches to secure the thread. Leave long threads at the beginning and end of rows, and pull the top thread through to the wrong side to tie it with the bobbin thread.

4. When the outlines of two channels cross each other, lift the pressure foot and needle and move the fabric forward so that you will not stitch on an area that is to be filled. A stitch in the middle of a channel will prevent the cording from passing through. (If you don't want a thread across the top of a channel, cut the threads and start a new line on the other side.)

5. Heavy or rough fabrics which are difficult to sew by hand can be done very

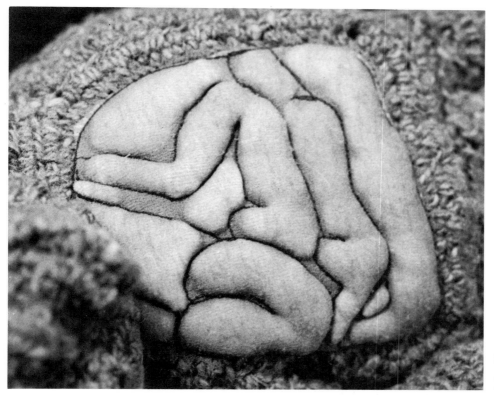

92. Machine stitching on jewelry. (Piece by Irene C. Reed)

easily on the machine. A strong backing fabric should be used with these materials (see pages 32–35 for information about backing fabrics).

6. When sewing the parallel lines for cording, in some cases you only need to draw the first of the two lines. For the second, you can gauge the distance by watching the pressure foot in relation to the first row of stitching.

Machine Stitching on Top Fabric Designs

If you are stitching a design that is on the top fabric, sew with standard-weight thread and a medium-length stitch. These stitches can be more decorative if contrasting or colored thread is used. (The spiderweb in photo 91 was sewn on the top fabric.) Use a tailor's chalk or very thin, light-lead pencil line to trace the design.

Machine Stitching on Backing Designs

To machine stitch a design that has been drawn on the backing fabric, use buttonhole twist in the bobbin, as it will be seen on the top fabric. Use a long stitch and adjust the tension if necessary.

QUILTING

Before the design can be raised, all of the quilting—the process of stitching around the design outlines—should be complete. You have a number of options in quilting, including the types of stitches you want to use and the amount of stitching you do on the piece. The stitching done in raised quilting allows as much room for creativity as the process of choosing the fabric and the design; here again, you should let your imagination have a free rein.

There are, of course, certain qualities any piece of needlework should have; and there are definite criteria used to judge raised quilting formally (a suggested scale for point judging is given on page 129), but they deal primarily with the way the finished piece looks. In this, as in any other type of needlework, you should consider not only the appearance but also the practical matters. For example, securing and tacking the ends of threads and closing the openings in the backing are technically important to the way a piece will last; but time and energy used to preen the underside of a piece that will not be seen are wasted.

In any event, your needlework should "pleasure" you.

Preparing the Piece for Quilting

1. Cut all layers of fabrics—top, backing, and optional middle layer of batting —to the desired size, leaving a seam allowance of at least ½ inch on all sides. The piece will "shrink" slightly and you'll lose some area when you quilt and raise the design, so allow for that also, if necessary. This is particularly important when you are making garments because the size and fit of the piece can be greatly altered by this loss. In addition to the normal seam allowance, leave an extra inch on all sides to compensate for it. (More details on cutting garments are given on pages 163–65.)

2. If you are working with a solid fabric, transfer the design to either the backing or the top fabric (see detailed instructions in the chapter on "Designs").

3. Place the top fabric face down on a smooth surface, and cover it with batting and backing. Smooth the layers.

4. Carefully pin or baste the layers together to keep the fabrics from slipping and the design from shifting as you work. The texture of fabrics and the size of the details in a design will determine the amount and closeness of the rows of pins or basting needed. For example, the lining of SiBonne, a very smooth fabric which tends to slip badly in handling, on the skirt in photo 195 had to be very thoroughly basted to the top fabric over the butterfly design. The hot mitt in photo 227, however, required only four or five pins to hold the fabrics in place, as the design and piece were small and the cotton backing did not slip much. If you use pins, pin at the corners, around the edges ½ inch from the border, and around all designs. Basting is actually better; the best way is to sew diagonally across or up and down the piece, covering the entire design area.

5. Follow the instructions for quilting and raising the designs on pages 84–127.

General Guidelines for Quilting

Where to Start Sewing

Whether you are working on a solid or a pre-designed fabric, start quilting as close to the center of the piece as possible, and work outward. Avoid skipping around, quilting one design in a corner, another in the center, and so forth. This prevents the backing from slipping and buckling the top fabric. In a pattern like the pineapple in photo 1, which has many tiny sections to be filled individually, start outlining the sections in the center of the pineapple, then quilt the next row, around the center, and so on, finishing with the stem and leaves. If you have one large design figure simply outline the entire figure, starting in the middle of the body and working all the way around.

When to Quilt Inner Design Details

At this point, if the piece is to be raised by stuffing, you have another decision: whether to quilt the inner detail lines of the design and stuff each area separately; or to wait until the stuffing is complete and *then* stitch the details through the fill. The latter will create a depression that is not as sharply defined as it would be if details were stitched and stuffed independently. You will have this problem more with a pre-designed fabric, since original designs tend to be simpler.

Generally, details of secondary importance are sewn *after* the stuffing has been added to give them secondary emphasis. Perhaps a simple example will make your choice easier. If the design has details within the main outline, like the flower on the left in photo 93, stuff the entire flower area, and then quilt the lines that define the petals, stitching through the stuffing. The overall flower will be more rounded than if the petal areas were outlined and stuffed individually. (This technique would also be used when the wing of a bird is folded against the body like the one in photo 94.)

On the other hand, in a design like the fully opened flower in photo 93, there are a number of equally important design elements. Each petal could be outlined and stuffed separately, giving all equal importance. The receding center of the flower would be outlined separately, but to give the flower more perspective, add less padding to this area than in the petals.

The type of design will also influence your choice. A stylized pattern, such as the quilt block in photo 44, will be more effective if the individual parts are outlined and raised separately; while a realistic design, like the flowers on the skirt in photo 193, will have a more natural, rounded form if the details are stitched after the filler material has been added.

93. When design has one main outline with inner detail lines like the flower on the left, quilt details after fill has been added. When there are several independent, or equally important, areas in the design, like the opened flower on the right, outline parts separately and then stuff.

94. For realistic designs like this bird, inner details should be quilted after stuffing is complete.

Ground, or Fill, Quilting

As its name implies, ground quilting is stitching that is used to fill in the background or flat areas around a raised design; and its uses are both functional and decorative. It is not always a necessary element of raised quilting; in fact, it can distract from the design, especially if it is used to fill the background when a layer of batting has been added. It is never done on top of raised areas. Normally, ground quilting is done in a running stitch, although in certain early pieces, particularly garments, a tight little back stitch was used.

In early trapunto, ground quilting was added to give more body to the article and to provide more warmth and protection to the wearer. The cap panel in photo 9 and the coverlet in photo 10 are good examples. Sometimes, to give even greater strength and warmth, cording was inserted between parallel rows of ground quilting, as was done in the Voorhees quilt in photo 14.

On larger articles, ground quilting is needed to hold the layers of fabric together; on smaller pieces and those where the design covers most of the surface, however, it is not necessary for that purpose.

As a decorative element, ground quilting is used to flatten the background, making the raised areas even more outstanding. In many bed quilts, like the coverlet in photo 15 and other large pieces, overall geometric ground quilting patterns traditionally were used to make borders and to fill areas not otherwise covered with a design.

Some of the best ground quilting patterns, of course, come from traditional quilting; and one of the most effective and versatile of these patterns is the diamond shape.

As in all geometrical patterns, the diamond has its own directional flow, which makes it particularly effective when used with rounded raised designs. When using this pattern, run the diagonal lines up to the edge of the design, stop, and then continue them on the other side. This produces the effect of a raised design lying on top of an overall diamond pattern background. Diamond ground quilting was used in the quilt blocks in photos 44 and 45. (Notice the difference in appearance of the ground-quilted areas between the piece with batting and the one with only two layers of fabrics.)

To produce other interesting effects, you can vary the size of the diamonds on the same piece. On the LOVE pillow in photo 95, the overall diamond pattern stops at the cording that outlines the letters and continues, on a smaller scale, within the letter "L."

A diamond pattern can be copied from many design sources, or you can make your own (instructions are given on page 70).

In lieu of the diamond, rows of parallel, diagonal lines can be used for ground quilting, which can be seen in the Hock quilt in photo 79.

Another traditional ground quilting design is the shell, or teacup, which was used on the coverlet in photo 78 and inside the letter "V" in the LOVE pillow (photo 96). (Instructions for making a shell pattern are given on pages 70–71.)

Other types of ground quilting have no patterns of their own; instead, they borrow from the outline of a raised design or simply wander in a free pattern.

Ground quilting which follows the outline of the design is sometimes termed a wave pattern, for it creates ripples like the ones around a rock thrown into a pond. It is quite easy to do; the lines don't even have to be drawn in if you have a good eye and watch the edge of the design or the last row you stitched. The effect produced by this type of ground quilting is to echo or magnify the central design, like the leopard design in the hot mitt in photo 97. The rows of stitches can be as close as you like; the closer the rows, the flatter and more "crepelike" the area becomes.

The free pattern, appropriately called meander stitching in traditional quilting, wanders around at random until an area is completely filled with stitches, although the line never touches or crosses itself. This technique was used inside the letter "E" on the LOVE pillow.

Ground quilting on a pre-designed fabric can be done by outlining though not stuffing some or all of the secondary designs. (This was done on the hot mitt in photo 227.) If the raised design is against a solid background and has a simple outline, you can use the wave pattern described before, following the outline of the printed design.

Unless your piece needs the extra stitches of ground quilting to hold the

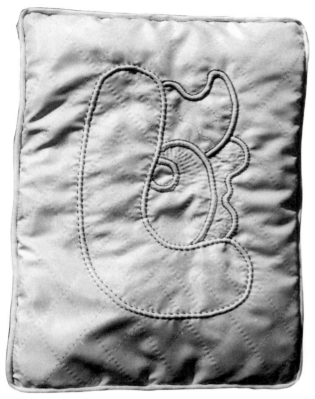

95. "LOVE" pillow, designed and worked by Mary Morgan, is a sampler of different ground quilting patterns.

96. A detail of the "LOVE" pillow shows the use of various ground quilting techniques: 1-inch diamonds fill the background outside the letters, continued inside the "L" as ½-inch diamonds; inside the "O" the ground quilting follows the outline of the letter; a small shell pattern is used inside the "V"; and the "E" is filled with a meander stitch.

fabric in place, you have a choice of using it or not. The decision doesn't have to be made until all of the outline quilting is done; however, ground quilting should be done before the designs are raised.

After all the quilting has been completed, remove the pins or basting, and you're ready to raise the design. If the piece has become wrinkled and mussed as you have quilted, iron it on the wrong side before stuffing or cording.

Curing Wrinkles and "Waves" in Finished Work

Sometimes you will run into the problem of having the top fabric and backing shift during quilting, creating an unfortunate effect of "buckling." There are ways to cure this, without having to take all the stitches out and requilt the piece.

If there is just a slight tightness in the backing that causes the problem, cut the backing under the wrinkled areas, in alternating slits. This will let the backing expand, releasing the tension and allowing the two layers to line up and not pull.

If the situation is quite bad, you may need to cut the entire backing away from around the design. Be careful not to cut close to the stitches or the fabric will ravel and pull loose.

97. Wave pattern ground quilting echoes the main design on this hot mitt.

Raising the Design

There are almost as many ways to raise a design as there are ways to do the stitching, and no one particular method is *the* right way. Some of the techniques given here are traditional; others are modern adaptations. All of them are offered primarily as suggestions to start you out in the right direction, for raising a design is as creative and individualistic as any other art form. It is, in fact, rather like sculpting, for you must mold and shape a design in fabric to suit your own tastes. You shouldn't hesitate to try your own ideas or any combination of the methods described here.

Be forewarned that because of the misapprehensions about trapunto, no matter how you do it, someone will probably say, "That's not the right way." But *they* are wrong, not you. There may be a quicker or easier way, or a more traditional method, than the one you've chosen, but if the finished piece suits you and anyone who is judging it, then it's the right way.

There are actually two basic methods of raising a design: by stuffing loose fill into the outlined area (trapunto), and by threading a cord through narrow channels of stitching (Italian quilting). A piece can be limited to one type of raising, or it can have a combination of the two techniques. The size and shape of the area, and your personal taste, will determine the method to use.

STUFFING

Stuffing a design area with loose fill material is probably the oldest form of raised quilting ever developed. Basically, the process is to make a hole in the backing material, within the stitched outlines of the pattern, and insert fill into the area to raise the design. The hole is made by cutting with scissors (cut-backing stuffing) or by separating the fibers with a pointed instrument (open-weave stuffing).

But there are other ways to stuff a design, as you will see in this chapter.

Materials for Stuffing

Practically speaking, most of your quilted pieces will need to be cleaned at least occasionally, if not regularly; and, therefore, a washable material is the best general fill. Most quilters prefer polyester for stuffing designs, as well as for quilt

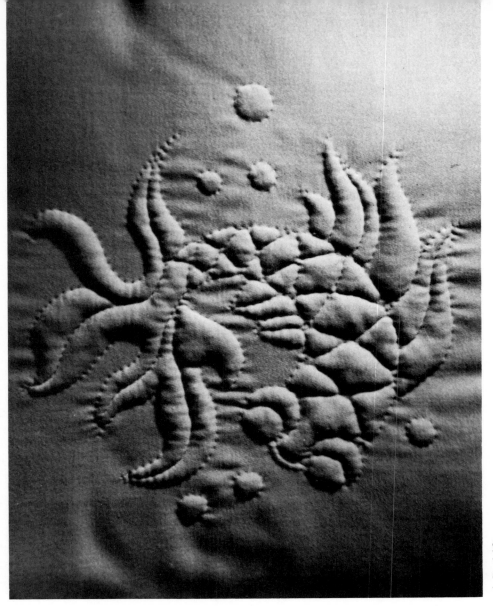

98. Fish design on cotton
velveteen, raised by
stuffing. Designed and
worked by Mary Morgan.

batting and fill for pillow forms. Besides being very resilient and easy to work with, polyester doesn't shrink or mat when laundered, won't absorb or hold moisture, and dries quickly. It comes in a loose form, called fill, and in layer form, called quilt batting. The latter is available in standard bed and crib sizes and can be used in a layer or easily cut or torn apart for use in general stuffing. Sometimes batting has a stiff surface treatment added to hold the fibers together; this should be peeled off before you use it for stuffing.

There is more than one kind of polyester fill, and though their basic characteristics are the same, there are differences in the way they handle and the appearance they give to the finished piece. Fine, short fibers make a fill that is softer, less resilient, and often less uniform than other polyesters. When using a light, soft fill, you may have a tendency to overstuff, which causes an unevenness and hardness in the padded areas. A fill made with longer, thicker fibers has more resilience, and less material is needed to raise an area. Nothing on the package will indicate these qualities, but a close scrutiny of the material through the plastic bag will help.

At this writing, the most commonly used American polyester fills are Dacron®, Mountain Mist®, and Fiber Fill®. In England, a polyester batting called Courtelle® is widely used, as it is inexpensive, easy to quilt, and easy to care for. Terylene® and Tricel® also work well.

Some wools and cottons make good fill materials, but they are not as practical as the synthetics for daily use articles and generally are not as easy to work with as their imitators. Neither of these fibers will retain its shape after cleaning as well as synthetics.

Cotton fill generally has less resilience than polyester and is more apt to lump when stuffed. In washing, it absorbs moisture, mats down, and dries slowly. When used as a quilt batting, it is harder to sew through than the synthetics. Standard cotton fill and batting, and a soft English cotton fill called Domette®, are the most commonly used cotton fills in trapunto today.

Wool for batting and fill has good resilience, packs evenly, and provides warmth if the raised areas are extensive enough. It may shrink, however, in laundering, and moths find it simply delicious! A washed and carded wool, which is quite pleasant and effective to work with, is used more in English quilting than American.

If your piece is a permanent work of art, of course, it's not likely that you will ever want, or need, to clean it. Almost anything can be used to stuff the design, from polyester fill to styrofoam. Craftspeople use a wide variety of fill materials, from down and kapok to foam rubber, flexible polyurethane and polystyrene pellets to lint collected from the washing machine filter, balls of cosmetic cotton, and the padding from pill bottles.

Tools for Stuffing

The only tools needed for stuffing designs are an instrument to make a hole in the backing and one to stuff the fill into the design area. Sometimes they are the same instrument.

For cut-backing stuffing, you need a pair of sharp-pointed scissors and a slender instrument, like an orange stick or nut pick, with which to insert the fill.

For open-weave stuffing, you need a sharp-pointed tool to separate the fibers of the backing fabric and to reclose them after the stuffing is complete, and another tool to insert the fill.

The common orange stick is an excellent all-around tool for trapunto; you can improve on it for open-weave stuffing by sharpening the thicker end into a real point (with a pencil sharpener, razor blade, or knife), shaving the thinner end down flat, and cutting a small notch in it (photo 99). This gives you a fine two-in-one tool: the pointed end to open the fibers and the notched end for stuffing the fill.

99. Orange stick with one end flattened and notched for easier stuffing.

Another good combination for this type of stuffing is a sharpened popsicle stick (which can be purchased in dime stores) for making the hole and a smooth, round wooden toothpick for inserting the fill. If you break off a tiny tip from one end of the toothpick, the rough edges will catch and hold the fill for stuffing even better than the notched orange stick.

Metal instruments, like nut picks, can be used, but wood is better because it will give more traction with the fill materials.

A small pair of embroidery scissors comes in handy in stuffing in a couple of ways. They can be used to cut a hole or to separate the fibers in a small design area, and also to push the fill into tiny corners that no other tool can get into (photo 100).

The trick is to make a hole larger than the instrument that is used for stuffing the fill into the area.

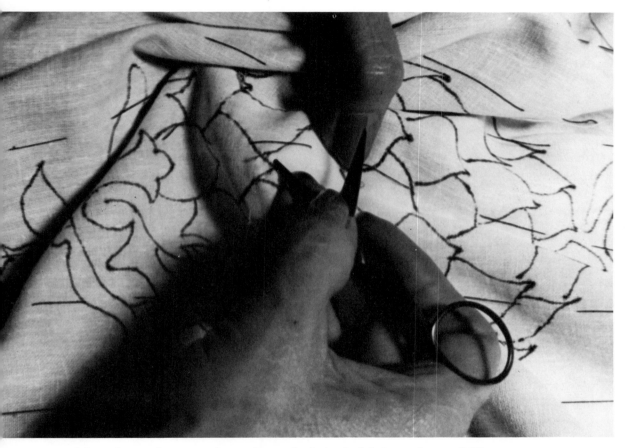

100. Tiny, sharp scissors can be used to make holes in fabrics and to stuff fill into small corners.

General Rules for Stuffing

The following suggestions apply to all types of stuffing:

1. Make sure that the fill is evenly distributed and not lumpy. Use the hand held under the piece to guide the fill, and for feeling to make sure it is not lumpy.

2. Don't overpack your design. Generally, very small areas (under ½ inch in diameter) should be packed fairly tightly; but larger areas should not be so tight

as to pull and distort the fabric around the padded area. Overstuffing an area where inner design details will be stitched through the fill will make the area rock hard and very difficult to sew through. (Many art pieces, however, are packed very tightly, to good effect, like the sample blocks on pages 26 and 27.)

3. Details within a raised area can be quilted after stuffing, using a stab stitch (page 78), or accented by small semi-back stitches (page 79) or other surface stitches that do not go through the fill.

Open-Weave Stuffing

The technique of using a pointed instrument to separate the fibers of the backing material without breaking them is referred to here as open-weave stuffing. This method would be used for fairly small design areas (less than 3 inches in diameter) and with backing fabrics that have a weave coarse enough to allow easy separation of the fibers. It would not work with a tightly woven backing.

1. Make a hole with a sharp instrument by holding the pointed end of the tool at an angle horizontal with the fabric. If you hold it straight up, you may punch a hole in the top fabric, too.

2. Push, twist, and wiggle gently until the weave separates. Remove the stick and you have a hole through which to do the stuffing.

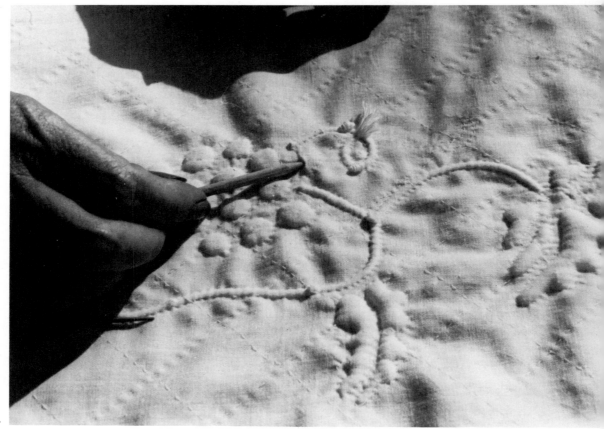

101.

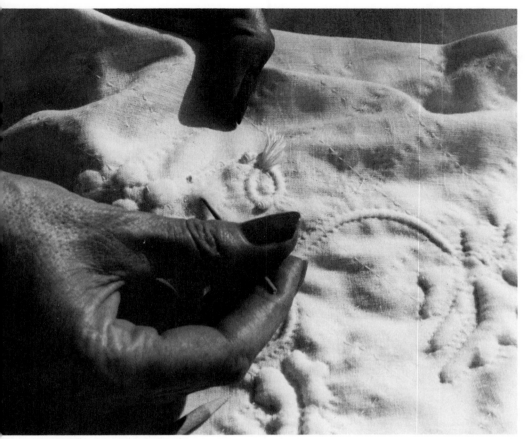

102.

3. Stuff the area with small pieces of loose fill, pushing them all the way to the edges of the design and filling the hard-to-reach areas with a pointed instrument. (See the general rules for stuffing on page 93.)

4. When the design has been stuffed, close the hole by using the pointed tool to push the threads gently back into place. If the back of the piece you are doing will be seen, the holes must be closed very carefully so that they will not be noticeable. (This is discussed further in the section on bed quilts, page 118.)

Cut-Backing Stuffing

The other way to open the backing fabric is by cutting a slit in it with a pair of pointed scissors (embroidery scissors work best).

1. The size of the slit will depend on the size of the area to be filled. Since you will close it eventually, make the opening large enough to be comfortable to work with, but don't cut close to the outline stitches.

2. Stuff the area, either with a pointed instrument or with your fingers (use the instrument to push the fill up to the edges of the outline and fill out the corners.)

3. After the area is filled, pull the edges of the cut backing together, without folding them over each other. Sew them together with large stitches, as in photo 103. (Some quilters prefer to tidy up the back with a close, more uniform stitch, and some substitute iron-on tape for stitches.) Dip down into the fill to help hold the stitches in firmly.

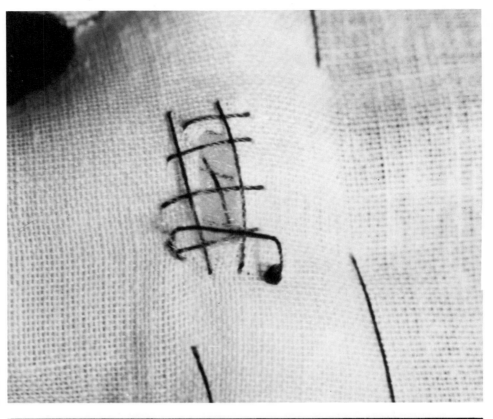

103. To close a hole after
stuffing, use long, loose
stitches.

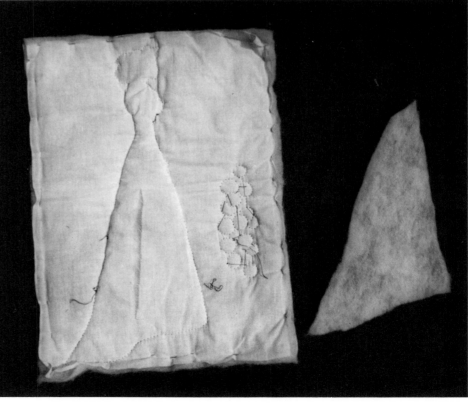

104. For large design areas,
layers of batting can be
cut the same size and
shape as the area to be
filled.

For stuffing a large area, you can cut a piece of batting the same size and shape as the area to be filled (photo 104). Work it into place with your hands through a very large slit. You can add more layers to raise the design even more.

Stuffing when using iron-on woven interfacing is a little tricky. In effect, you are working with a single layer of fabric that is made up of two layers held together by a bonding agent. Making a hole in the backing fabric without damaging the top fabric is the hard part. To do this, slide a pin between the layers and gently separate the fabrics. Make a space large enough to insert the tips of very pointed scissors so you can cut a slit in it. The two pieces of fabric will separate as you push the fill to the edges of the design. This technique eliminates basting, but it has some definite disadvantages. Try a small piece first.

"Outline" Stuffing

A design can also be stuffed by leaving a small opening of about 1 inch in the quilted outline and inserting the fill through this opening. To keep the fill in place, the outline stitching is completed after the stuffing is done. This method, however, is not highly recommended for it has a number of disadvantages for hand sewing. It is really good only for large, simple designs, with few individual areas to be raised.

Padding

This is a way to raise a design without opening the backing, although the end results are basically the same as in regular stuffing. Padding, which is strictly our own name for this method, is particularly handy for raising large design areas. (It was used on the angel wall hanging in photo 69 and the designs on the skirt in photo 194.)

1. Place a layer of batting, slightly larger than the design, between the top and backing fabrics, covering the design. Quilt the design outline, through all layers.

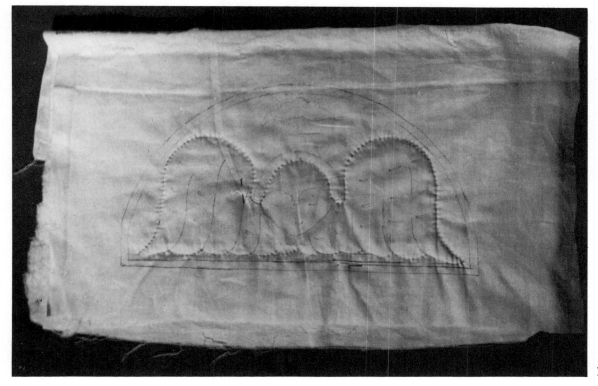

105.

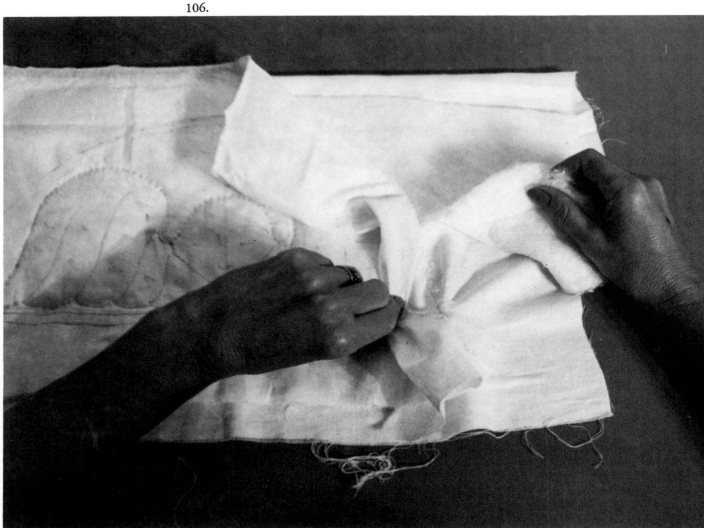

2. Lift the backing fabric and tear away the padding outside the stitches. If the padding is difficult to tear, snip it very carefully with scissors, making sure that you don't snip the top fabric too. (You may wish to use cotton batting because the fibers are shorter and it tears more easily than polyester; however, it mats down more easily than polyester and should not be used on pieces that will be "pressed" repeatedly, like a pillow.)

3. You can add even more fill to the area later, of course, in the conventional manner. On this particular piece (the angel rubbing wall hanging), other smaller independent design areas—the cloud over the head, for example—were stuffed through a hole in the backing.

CORDING, OR ITALIAN QUILTING

The most expedient way to raise a narrow design area formed by parallel rows of stitching (a stem of a flower or a geometric design, for example) is to thread a narrow piece of material like yarn or soft cording through the channel created by the stitches. Normally, this technique is done on two layers of material—top and backing—and is referred to as Italian quilting. The same raised effect can be achieved, however, by attaching the cord to the back of a single layer of material. The oval design (photo 108) was done on a single layer, while the other figures were worked on the traditional two layers.

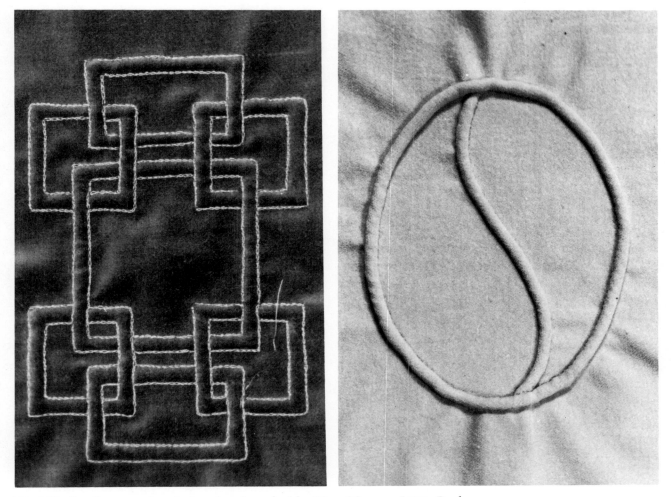

107, 108. Cording sampler, designed and worked by Mary Morgan. LEFT: Dark brown velveteen with chain stitch in gold metallic thread; cording on two layers of fabric, design marked on top fabric with white tailor's chalk. Design adapted from an advertisement in a newspaper. (Design for transfer in fig. 48.) RIGHT: Beige velveteen with cross-over back stitch in contrasting-colored buttonhole twist; single layer of fabric.

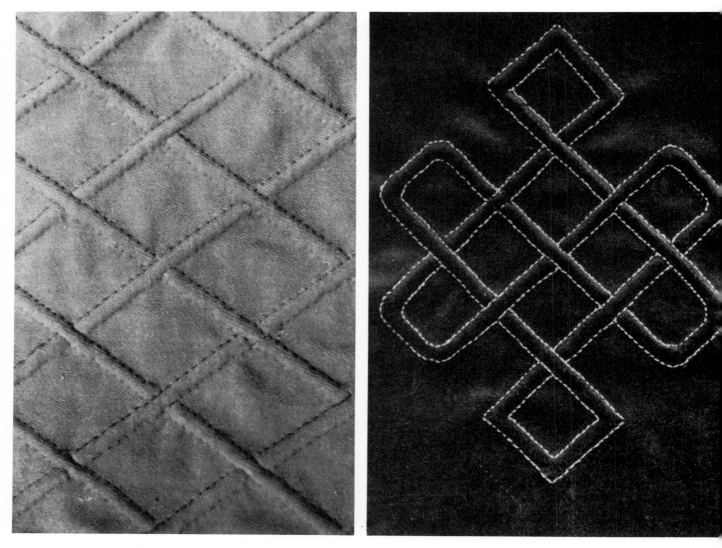

109, 110. LEFT: Beige velveteen with running stitch in silk thread; two layers of fabric; design transferred to backing. RIGHT: Brown velveteen with short back stitch in buttonhole twist thread; two layers of fabric; design transferred to top fabric. All pieces raised with polyester cable cord. (Design for transfer in fig. 49.)

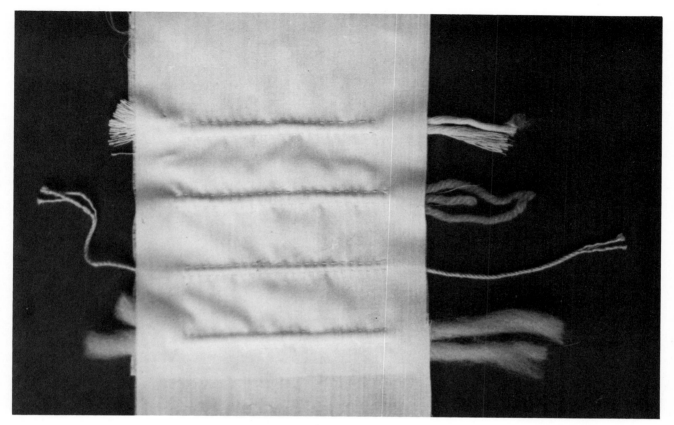

Materials for Cording

The term "cording" also refers to the material which is threaded through the channel design. There are a number of materials that can be used, including yarn, piping, cord of various types, twine, mason's line, and even candlewick, which is found in early pieces like the quilt in photo 79.

A consideration in choosing the cording material is the use of the article. If it needs to be cleaned often, a washable cording is best; and if the piece is to be handled very much, remember that a hard cord will wear out the fabrics faster than a soft one.

The best all-around material is a polyester cable cord. It's washable, won't shrink or stretch, dries quickly, and is not too hard. Available in fabric shops, cable cord comes in a number of different thicknesses consisting of several twisted strands which can be separated to fit any size channel.

Normally we start with ¼-inch cable cord (No. 150) and untwist it into four smaller strands (photo 112). You can get rid of twists and tangles by running your finger down the cord as you separate the strands. To fill a standard ¼-inch channel, use one of these strands *doubled* (threading it through the needle doubles it). A little simple arithmetic will help determine how much cording to buy for a piece: one of the unraveled strands 30 inches long, for example, will fill a 15-inch-long channel; so, a piece of ¼-inch cable cording 30 inches long will fill four times that much, or 60 inches of channel.

Note: Any cording should be unwound if the lines of the twist show through the top fabric.

111. Materials used in cording (from top to bottom): polyester cable cord, worsted yarn, butcher cord, Italian quilting wool.

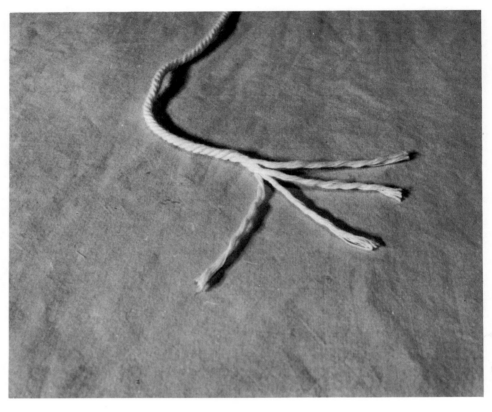

112. No. 150 cable cord being separated into four equal strands for cording.

Worsted knitting yarns, especially those of synthetic fibers, are excellent, because you can easily add more strands to fit different-size designs. Yarn has more resilience than cable cord and will fill a soft fabric without packing too hard. It does have a tendency to stretch, however, a quality that some quilters do not like. Colorful synthetic yarns for gift-tying are quite good for use in shadow quilting (page 121). Its laundering qualities are questionable, so it is best used for art pieces that won't need to be washed.

Wool yarn and Italian quilting wool (available in England) are both fine, though not as easy to care for as the synthetics.

Cotton cording is satisfactory, but if you intend to machine wash the piece, the cording should be pre-shrunk by dropping it into a pan of boiling water and simmering for 5 minutes.

Other materials that can be used are the traditional wax candlewick and butcher cord, which is good for raising designs on a heavy or thick material. Welting is not particularly suitable because it is covered with a fine mesh that will show through top fabrics; also, it cannot be separated and is difficult to thread into a bodkin.

For artwork, literally anything can be used, since shrinkage from laundering is of no consequence.

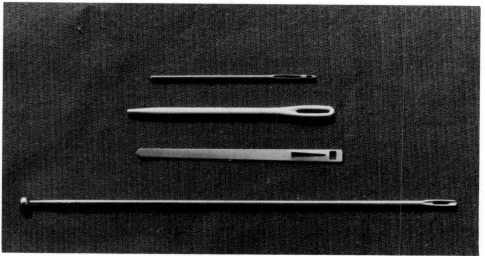

113. Tools for cording (from top to bottom): embroidery needle, bodkin (plastic yarn needle), tape threader, long ball threader.

Tools for Cording

To pull a cord through a channel design, you need a blunt needle with an eye large enough for the thick material. A number of different instruments are suitable, some of which are shown in photo 113. Tapestry and wool needles and bodkins are very good; and they come in several eye sizes, in both metal and plastic.

114.

To speed your work, you can quickly make a needle-threader (for yarn) this way:

1. Make a loop of regular thread and insert it through the eye of the needle or bodkin (photo 114).

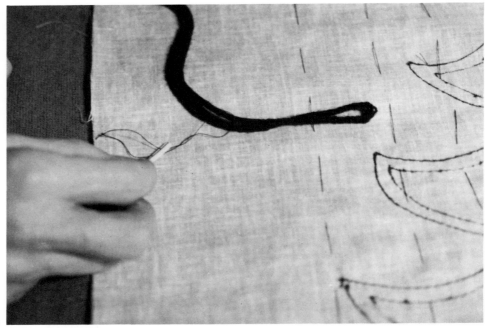

115.

2. Put the yarn through the loop.

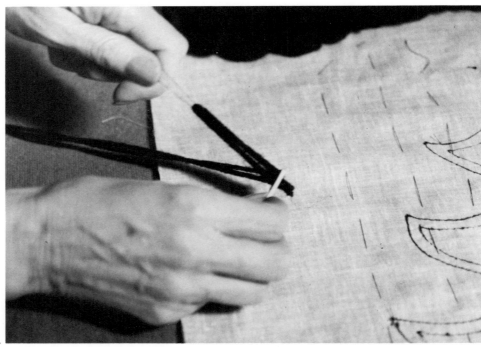

116.

3. Pull both loop and yarn back through the eye of the needle.

A long "ball"-type threader (made for threading elastic through bands and so forth) can also be used for cording. Tie the cord to it with a strong thread. This instrument is particularly good for those times when you use a very thick cord, such as in the child's play sheet (photo 211).

117. Underneath side of butterfly corded on two layers of fabric.

Cording with Two Layers of Material—Italian Quilting

1. Thread a bodkin or other blunt needle. Determine the thickness of the cording or yarn by the size and shape of the channel to be filled. It's best to test the channels for proper cording size in a sample (or unused corner) of your material before deciding on the thickness to be used. It's exasperating to find that your cording is so thick that you need pliers to pull it through the channel or that the cording is not thick enough to raise the design properly.

118.

2. Turn the piece face down and make a hole in the channel without breaking the fibers, or by cutting the backing. Start at the end of a channel or a corner, if possible.

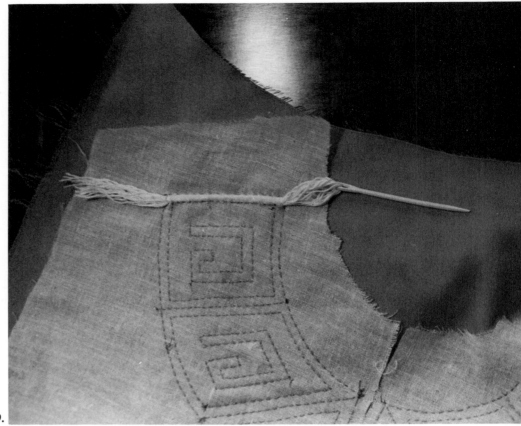

119.

3. Pull the cording through the channel.

4. If the channel is straight, run the cording all the way through, come out at the end or a sharp corner, and cut the cord, leaving ½ inch sticking out at each end. (If you are using a fairly thin strand of wool, you can simply leave a small loop at the corner, re-enter the channel, and continue, rather than cutting the cord.)

5. When filling a curved channel, bring the needle out when it has gone as far as it can without twisting the fabric. Re-insert the needle in the same hole, and leave a small loop where it comes out. This loop is left when you are using yarn so the fabric will not be pulled or wrinkled, as the yarn "shrinks" when it is no longer being pulled (taut) through the channel. Polyester cable cording does not stretch like yarn, so normally you can clip the loop after cording is complete.

6. If two channels cross each other, one cord should not be carried over or under the other. Come out of the channel at the crossing, cut the cord, leaving ½ inch, and start again on the other side.

7. When all channels have been filled, stretch the piece gently on the bias. The loose ends can be cut close to the fabric; and loops, if they show through the top fabric, can be cut in the center and trimmed. Yarn may work back into the channel, so don't trim it too close to the fabric.

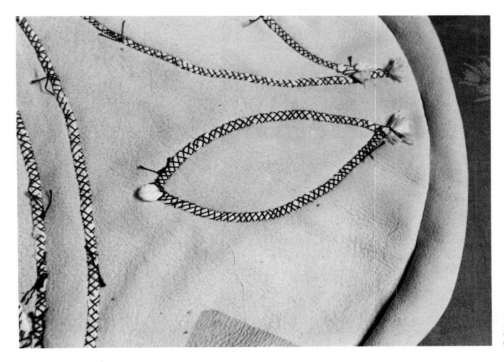

120. Underneath side of pillow design showing cross-over back stitch.

Cording on One Layer of Material

This is a good way to raise designs and monograms on linen and heavier fabrics like chamois. In some ways it is easier than regular cording, for there is no backing to slip in the process of stitching. Parallel lines are drawn on the top side of the fabric, and a cord is held in place underneath it.

1. Bring the needle up from the underside, coming out at point A. Pull the thread all the way through the fabric, and insert it at B, a stitch-length behind A. Bring it under the cord, at an angle, and come up at C on the other side, just opposite A (fig. 16). Pull the thread all the way through.

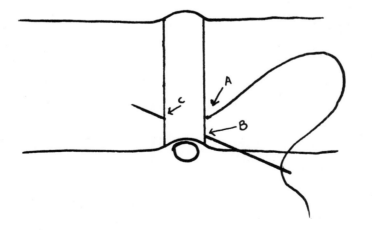

Fig. 16.

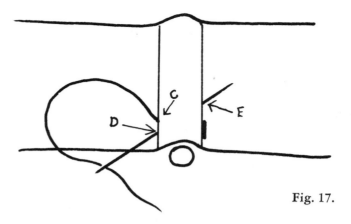

Fig. 17.

2. Insert the needle at D, a stitch-length behind C, and bring it under the cord and out at E (fig. 17). Pull it all the way through. These two stitches create an "X" under the cord. Continue in this manner, and you will create a series of "Xs" under the cord to hold it in place.

121. "Appliquéd smile" on blue jeans. Designed by Robert Alan Gary, worked by Mary Morgan.

RAISED APPLIQUÉ

The addition of filler material to raise an appliquéd piece is not a new idea; it is really the same principle that was used in the seventeenth- and eighteenth-century needle art form called stump work. Today, craftspeople and artists use these techniques to do fantastic wall hangings, pillows, soft sculpture, and so on, incorporating trapunto and appliqué.

122. "County Fair," trapunto picture by Deanna Glad, appliquéd, stuffed. Made of a variety of fabrics, backed with felt; kapok fill. (Photo courtesy of the artist)

123. "Via Matisse," wall hanging by Lenore Greenfield. Excellent example of artwork done in appliqués and raised work. Polyester and cotton.

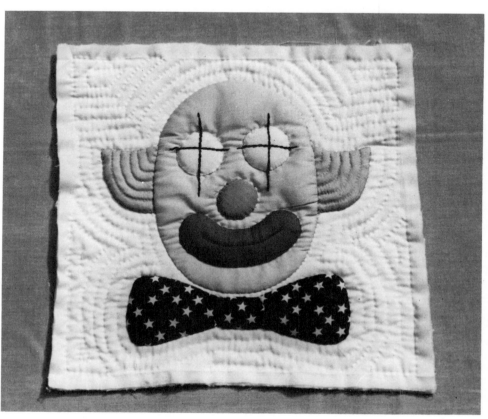

124. Clown face, appliquéd quilt block, designed and worked by Mary Morgan.

There are several ways to raise an appliqué. The clown quilt block in photo 124 is given here as an example, for it utilizes two of the most common techniques. Patterns and complete instructions for assembling and finishing the piece are also given so that you can make your own Clara Bell Clown, as a quilt block, a decorator pillow, or a wall hanging.

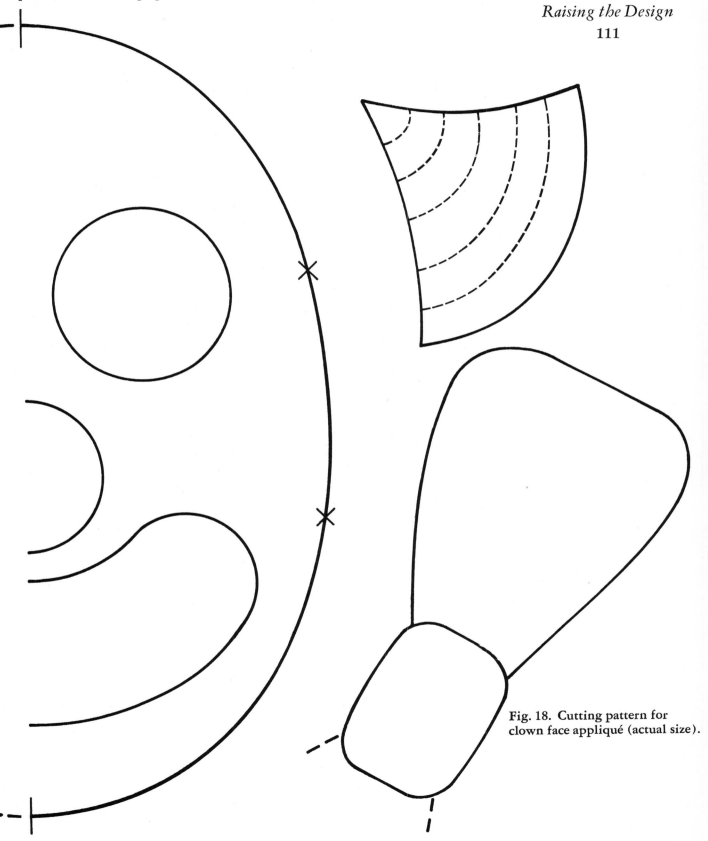

Fig. 18. Cutting pattern for clown face appliqué (actual size).

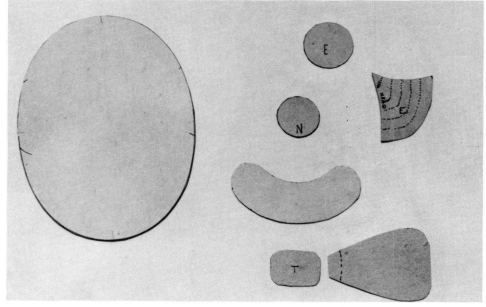

125.

1. Trace the entire design (fig. 18) on paper, with lines dark enough to be seen through the fabric.

2. Make patterns (templates) from cardboard for each piece to be appliquéd: head, nose, mouth, one eye, one side and center of the bow tie, and one hairpiece (photo 125).

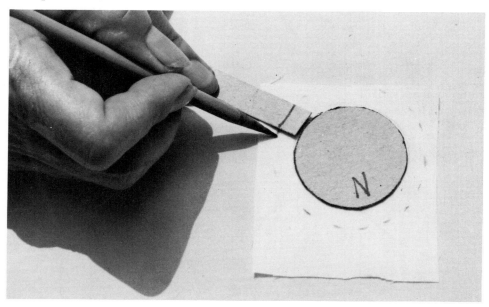

126.

3. Use a sharp No. 2 lead pencil to outline the templates on the fabrics chosen for each appliqué. Add a ¼-inch seam allowance all around. (Be sure to cut two each of the eye, bow tie, and hairpiece.) Fold the material before cutting the tie and hair so that you don't end up with two pieces for the same side of the face (photo 126).

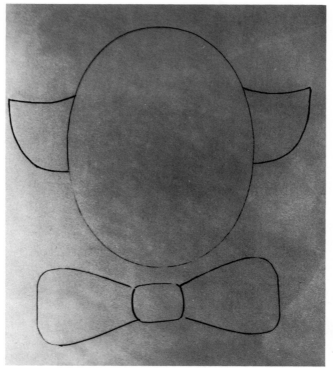

127.

4. Cut out the appliqués.

5. Clip all curved edges every ¼ inch up to, not through, the pencil line.

6. Cut out a square piece of material (referred to as the ground fabric). The piece shown was cut 12 × 12 inches. Trace the outline of the head, hair, and bow tie from the original design onto it (photo 127).

7. Trace the outlines of eyes, nose, and mouth on the face appliqué, from the original design.

8. The hair appliqués will be corded, so cut a backing for each. Trace the dotted lines for stitching on the backing, and baste to the top fabric. Use a running stitch to outline the channels and cord them with several strands of worsted-weight yarn. (Don't use too much yarn or it will distort the shape of the piece; it should lie flat when finished.) Trim the cording back to the seam allowance.

128.

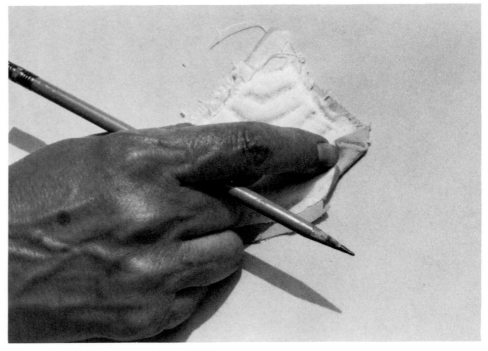

129.

9. Turn the seam allowance on the hairpiece under, iron, and baste to hold it down. To make sharp corners, turn first one side under, and then the other, overlapping the two edges.

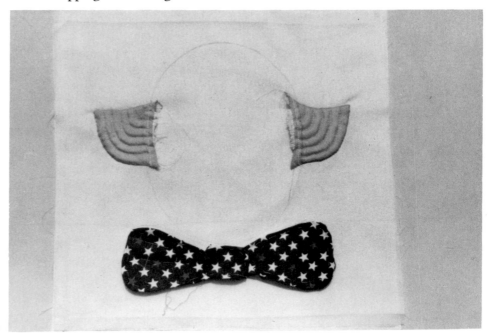

130.

10. Appliqué the hairpieces to each side of the head on the ground fabric, as marked on the pattern by "Xs." Make small, close blind stitches, using thread that matches the color of the appliqué material.

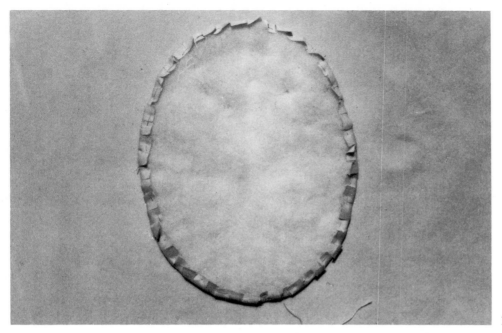

131.

11. To raise the face, cut out a layer of quilt batting the same shape but slightly smaller than the appliqué. Place the appliqué face down, cover it with the batting, and fold the clipped edges over the batting. Baste it to hold the seam allowance down.

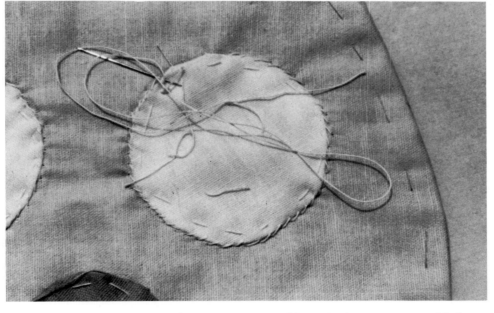

132.

12. Raise the mouth and the three pieces of bow tie the same way, with layers of batting behind the appliqués.

13. Appliqué the necktie to the ground fabric.

14. Turn under the seam allowance of the eyes and nose, and appliqué the pieces to the face, leaving an opening in the seam of about ½ inch (photo 132).

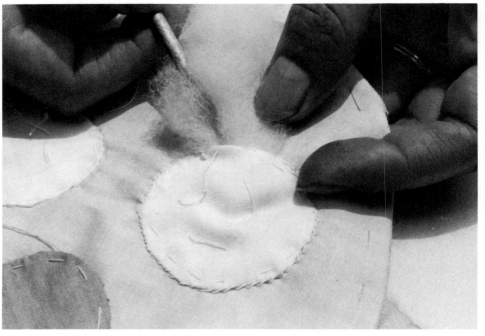

133.

15. Insert small amounts of fill through the openings until the eyes and nose are lightly padded. Finish the seams.

134.

16. Appliqué the mouth to the face.

17. Appliqué the face to the corresponding outline on the ground fabric.

18. Use an embroidery stem stitch to decorate the eyes and mouth, catching only the top layer of fabric.

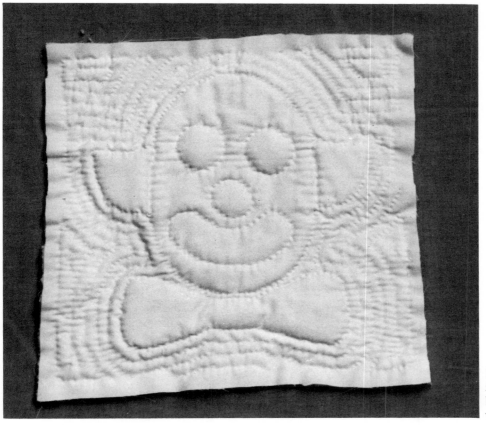

135. **Back side of clown face after batting and backing have been added, with ground quilting.**

19. This Clara Bell was finished as a quilt would be by adding a layer of batting and a back of woven broadcloth (to match the top fabric) to the underside of the quilted piece. Ground quilting in a running stitch in rows that follow the outlines of the head, eyes, nose, and mouth was added. This holds the batting and back in place and puts more emphasis on the clown's face and its features. (Of course, if you used this as a quilt block, you would sew all of the quilted blocks together and *then* add batting and back over the entire area, and do the ground quilting.) You can add the ground quilting to emphasize the design, even if you do not make this into a pillow or wall hanging.

Raised appliqués can also be added to ready-made items, like the blouse in photo 136. To coordinate the blouse with a pre-designed skirt, flowers were cut from fabric remnants, appliquéd, and raised on the blouse. To add an appliqué of this sort:

136. **Ready-made blouse with pre-designed chintz appliqués. Stitched with silk thread, stuffed.**

1. Cut out the design, leaving a ¼-inch seam allowance all around.

2. Clip the edges, as in step 5 of the clown instructions. Press under and baste.

3. Appliqué to the garment, leaving a ¾-inch opening in the stitching to add the fill.*

4. Add fill and complete the stitching. Depress inner details, through the fill, with a stab stitch. (On this particular design, stems were appliquéd separately and raised with cording.)

Art-type appliqués, like the smile on the blue jeans in photo 121, and the elephant in photo 3, are added to a piece in the same basic way. To make the smile appliqué:

1. Transfer the design to appliqué fabric. Cut it out, leaving a ¼-inch seam allowance. Clip the edges as in step 5 of the clown instructions.

2. Quilt the center lines of the lips to the garment with a running stitch. (This area will remain flat.)

3. Appliqué the edges to the garment, adding fill to the small, hard-to-reach areas as you sew. (Do not stuff hard enough to distort the fabric.) Before completing the outline, add fill to the whole area, and finish stitching.

4. The teeth are added with large overcast stitches using white embroidery thread.

RAISING A DESIGN ON A BED QUILT

No book on any type of quilting is quite complete without a word on bed quilts. The very word "quilt" connotes a bed coverlet, usually one with elaborately stitched designs. And many of the surviving examples of early trapunto and Italian quilting are found on European and American quilts—so, contemporary raised work owes much to these early bed coverings.

Old bed quilts are lovely in both design and execution, but to a trapunto quilter, the most amazing aspect is how well the openings made for the stuffing have been hidden. Often, the holes were reclosed so well you can't tell where the padding was added even with very close inspection.

Making a quilt is a complicated task, and you'll need more instructions than we can give in a book of this nature. There are many good books on how to construct a quilt, so the suggestions here are limited to ways of raising designs on articles where the back will be seen. The techniques described, then, apply to bed quilts and other articles as well.

There are several ways to end up with a neat back which doesn't look pockmarked from the holes made to accommodate stuffing or have unsightly closing stitches, thread ends, and knots.

1. Use a coarsely woven backing fabric, such as a 100 percent cotton muslin sheet, which can be opened with a pointed instrument without breaking the fibers and closed to the original arrangement without showing. Extremely coarse backing was the secret of the early quilters' success; but this is not the best solution for modern quilters. Today's fabrics are of finer weave and many

* You can also sew the appliqué on completely and make a hole behind the appliqué in the garment, providing you don't plan to remove it some day. (Adding an appliqué is a handy way to cover a hole, by the way.)

137. "The Sea Is Me," trapunto quilt by Elsa Brown, made of polyester/nylon semi-sheer fabric. Machine stitched and stuffed. (Photo courtesy of the artist)

138. Trapunto coverlet by Bonnie Johnson. Central butterfly is an original design; bows in each corner and on piece attached to cover pillow are from a Mountain Mist® quilting pattern. Made of purple corduroy with lightweight cotton backing.

139. Detail from the "Great Quilt," designed and executed by a group of artists, shows one block using raised appliqué. Design of a malted milkshake commemorates a malted drinking contest. Designed and worked by Mr. Wines and Alison Sky. (By permission of Marilynn Gelfman-Pereira Karp)

have a resin finish, which is why they have highly desirable handling and laundering qualities but are unsuitable for open-weave stuffing.

If you use this method, you also need to hide your thread ends and knots, and there are a couple of ways to do this. One is to make tiny knots, which can be gently tugged through the coarse backing and caught between layers of fabric. Another is to insert the needle with an unknotted thread 1 inch away from where you wish to begin stitching. Go between the layers and come out (on top) where you want to start the quilting outline. Leave a little thread sticking out of your original entry spot. Make one or two small back stitches at the beginning of the outline to secure the thread, and start your row of stitching. Cut the beginning thread flush with the fabric.

To end a row without showing threads or knots, make one or two small back stitches* to secure thread; insert needle between the layers of fabric, and come out 1 inch away from the last stitch. Cut thread flush with fabric.

2. Another way is to do quilting and stuffing in the normal manner, using a top fabric and backing only. When complete, line the piece with a third layer of material—a back that will hide stitches, holes, and thread ends.

You can also add a layer of batting between the quilted top piece and the back. Layers must be held together, perhaps by ground quilting through all layers. This way, the original outline quilting around raised designs will not be seen on the back, but the ground quilting will. Bury the knot according to the instructions given in method 1. This technique is demonstrated in the clown face in photo 124.

* If these stitches are to be used around an area that will be stuffed or corded, two back stitches at the beginning and end will secure the thread better.

SPECIAL TECHNIQUES FOR RAISING DESIGNS

There are certain methods of raising designs that don't exactly fit into either of the two basic techniques, stuffing and cording. These special methods produce some interesting relief effects and therefore are included to provide you with more options for doing raised quilting.

Shadow Quilting

The term "shadow quilting" is applied to any type of raised piece—stuffed or corded—in which the fill material clearly shows through the top fabric. The pieces on pages 121 and 123 are examples of this "see-through" raising.

A semi-transparent top fabric, like organza, is used over a backing, and any method of raising can be used. The profile pillow in photo 158 has both cording and stuffing; the iceberg in photo 140 was done by "padding"; and the birds (photo 141) were stuffed with cording (instructions follow). The fill material can be white, like the faces on the profile pillow, or of a contrasting color, like the cording that outlines the faces, so that it will show through even more.

An interesting variation is to use a darker color for backing material with a light top fabric and fill. This was used on the bridesmaid cap (photo 210), the faces on the purse in photo 142, and the soft sculpture in photo 143. When a darker backing fabric shows through between the stitching and fill, especially, the shadow effect gives even more emphasis to the design.

In the iceberg wall hanging, white organza was used as a top fabric over a backing of blue and green cotton. A second piece of white organza hangs free over the entire piece, creating a moiré pattern that gives a feeling of the frosty, cold atmosphere in the world of icebergs and polar bears.

140. "Iceberg" wall hanging, shadow quilting . Backing of green and blue cotton broadcloth (for sea and sky), top fabric of organza, with a second layer of organza hanging free over the entire piece to create a moiré effect by Mary Morgan.

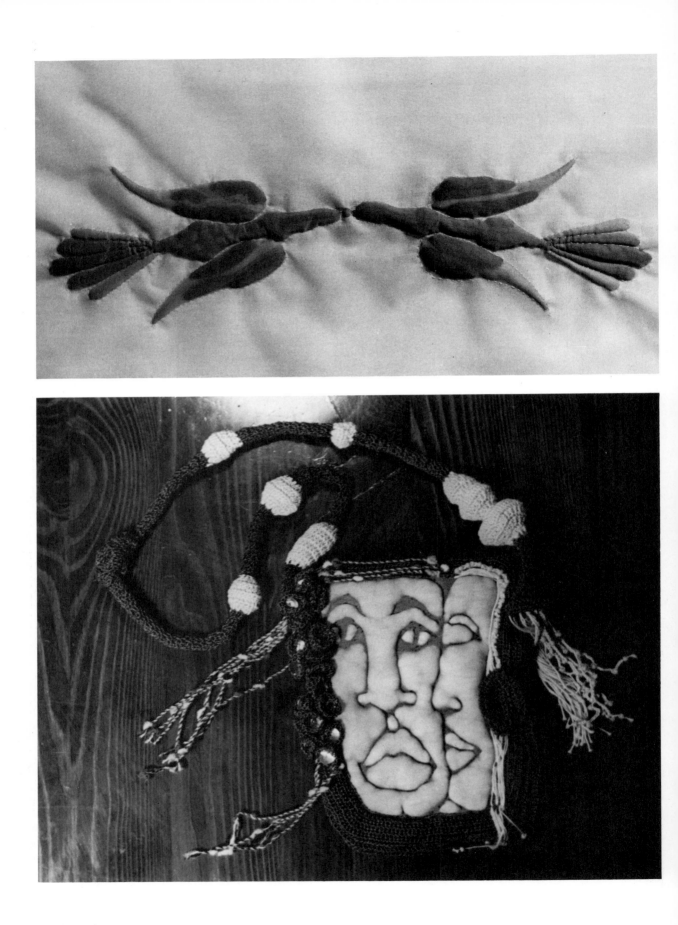

141. OPPOSITE, TOP: "Love Birds," wall hanging by Mary Morgan, is done with shadow quilting effects. Backing of white broadcloth with semi-transparent nylon top fabric, through which can be seen green and blue yarn used to raise the figures. Original design adapted from colorful bird pattern. Design for transfer in fig. 47.

142. OPPOSITE, BOTTOM: Bag by Irene C. Reed gets its stunning appearance from shadow effect.

143. BELOW: "Cloud Ladies with Sun," soft sculpture by Elsa Brown, is done by shadow quilting. Off-white semi-sheer polyester/nylon top fabric, over black polyester/cotton voile backing, with polyester fill. Machine stitched. (Photo courtesy of the artist)

Filling Irregular-Shaped Designs with Cording

To tell the truth, this technique was included in the "special" section because it is difficult to decide whether it belongs to stuffing or cording! In effect, it is a stuffing technique, using cording material to raise the design. The Love Birds in photo 141 were done by this method, incorporating shadow quilting effects. Raising with cording is a quick, easy way to fill small, irregular design areas.

1. Working from the back, insert a needle (threaded with yarn or very soft cording) on one side of the design area, just inside the outline stitches. Bring it all the way across the design and come out, again just inside the outline stitches on the opposite side.

2. Leave a small loop outside, and re-insert the needle close to the place you just came out. Bring it across the design and come out next to the original entry.

3. Repeat this process, going back and forth, until the area is filled.

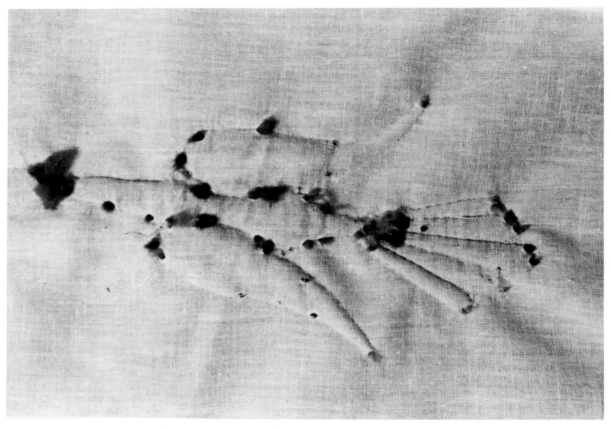

144.

4. Trim the ends of the yarn.

Raising Monograms

Monograms are a very special and personal way to use raised quilting on garments, pillows, bed coverlets, or furnishings. And with the wide variety of shapes and sizes available, letters afford an effective, diversified design group for trapunto. Lettering suitable for all methods of raising can be found in many places. There are commercial stencils and iron-on transfer patterns for lettering and whole books

145. The letter "P" from Butterick pattern No. 3970. Cording on single layer of handkerchief linen, done in silk buttonhole twist.

146. Back side of letter "P" shows cross-over back stitch used to hold cording in place.

devoted just to different types of letters. If you can find one, a printer's sample book of typefaces is a real prize possession. But interesting lettering is everywhere: on billboards and signs; in books, magazines, and newspapers; on packaging, car bumper stickers, and all manner of printed material.

Raising a letter is like raising any other design, and the same considerations in choosing fabrics, stitches, and techniques apply. The size and shape of the letters, and your own personal taste, will determine whether you raise with cording or by stuffing.

The technique most highly recommended is cording on a single layer of fabric, using the cross-over back stitch (pages 107–8). The "P" in photo 145 was done by this method. The main advantages are that the cross-over back stitch holds the cording for a small design securely in place, even in cleaning and handling; and this technique eliminates the need for a backing material which might add unwanted bulk to a garment and show up through a thin fabric as an ugly "patch."

Monograms can be raised also on two layers of material by either cording or stuffing, of course. The two "Rs" in photos 147 and 148 were done by cording. In both cases, a very coarsely woven backing fabric was used, and the cording was done by separating the fibers to make a hole in the backing. With a small design of this type, there is a possibility of the cording working out of the fabric through the holes; therefore, it's a safeguard to sew up the opening as you would in cut-backing stuffing to prevent this from happening in handling. (Instructions for cording on two layers are given on page 105.)

The two "Rs" demonstrate other important points to consider in raising monograms. Both were done on the same fabric (broadcloth), with the same material for raising (polyester cable cord). But the "R" in photo 147, done in solid back stitch outline with silk buttonhole twist, shows up much better than the second "R," which was done in a finer cotton thread with a broken outline running stitch. Also, the script-type "R" (photo 147), with its serif embellishments, has a more dramatic appearance than the sans-serif type in the second "R."

147. Script-type iron-on transfer of the letter "R." Cording done on two layers—top fabric of a blend of 65 percent polyester/35 percent cotton, backing of coarse-weave cotton. Quilted in back stitch with silk buttonhole twist.

148. Sans-serif "R," iron-on transfer. Cording done on two layers—top fabric of 65 percent polyester/35 percent cotton, backing of coarse-weave cotton. Quilted in running stitch with quilting thread.

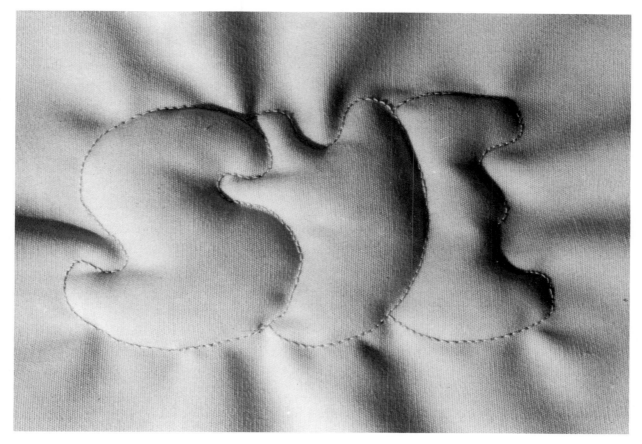

149. Balloon lettering designed by Mary Morgan.

Thicker letters can be raised by either open-weave (page 94) or cut-backing stuffing (page 95), like any other thick or rounded design. The fat balloon letters that spell "SUE" in photo 149 were raised by cut-backing stuffing. A letter doesn't have to be quite *that* thick, however, to be effectively stuffed rather than corded. A different appearance can be achieved by outlining thick letters with a row of cording, leaving the inside unraised, as was done in the "LOVE" pillow in photo 95. Or outline a letter with cording and stuff the center, too.

Special Hints

NOTES ON TEACHING CHILDREN AND "RANK AMATEURS" HOW TO DO TRAPUNTO

These suggestions grew out of an experience the author had while teaching a five-year-old granddaughter how to do a trapunto pillow. After instructing adults in the art of raised quilting for many years, the teacher learned a few lessons herself! Parents, grandparents, and teachers may be able to use the techniques that came out of this double learning experience to introduce children to needlecraft. These suggestions for helping a child learn can also apply to a rank amateur or a person who claims to be "all thumbs."

1. Start the child out with the simplest designs, quilting stitches, and raising techniques. For this project, a pre-designed fabric with a small, well-defined pattern was chosen, and a running stitch and open-weave stuffing were used. A larger needle than is normally used for quilting was threaded with a short length (10 inches) of doubled and pre-knotted thread. (Learning to knot a thread can come later.) A larger needle is easier for a child or inexperienced person to hold, and a short thread prevents snarling and strain on short arms.

2. To begin, the teacher cuts and works up one block as a guide to show the child what to do, step by step. (All demonstrations should be done only on the teacher's block.) The child watches while the teacher does one step, then she or he follows the example on her own piece.

3. The first goal is to outline one design completely. This may take two sessions as the attention span of a youngster is short. The stitches at first will be long and uneven, but as an "ease of stitching" is achieved, they will begin to look better. Demanding short and even stitches in the beginning can and will distress a young sewer—don't expect or ask for perfection. Remember, you want to develop a joy and pleasure in handwork. (After a running stitch is mastered, the child can learn to do a back stitch.)

4. It will make things easier if you show the child how to rest his or her arms on her knees or a pillow in her lap, as it will help to steady the work, and smaller, more even stitches will come more quickly.

5. When the outline is complete, the teacher makes an opening with a pointed instrument in the backing of her demonstration block, while the child watches. (If the child is very young, he or she is apt to cut through the top fabric if scissors are used to make the hole.)

6. Don't be surprised if on the fourth or fifth block the child insists on threading her own needle and choosing the length of thread. And you'll be pleased to see the progress between the first and fifth block; it's nice to number them on the back as they are completed.

7. Let the child arrange the blocks for a pillow top. The last block made in this piece (the best) went in the center.

8. Machine stitch the blocks together, while the child watches. How exciting it is to see the pieces come together!

9. Follow the instructions on page 135 for finishing a knife-edge pillow. It's fun for the child to sign and date the pillow (in India ink) on the back—just like a "real" artist.

In this case, it wasn't until she had done the third block that the granddaughter became interested enough to work without being urged. But when she saw the last block, and the finished pillow, she was full of ideas of her own about making doll pillows and pincushions for gifts. This made the sewing less of a game and more of a goal-oriented experience though it became more fun when real goals were in sight.

One last reminder: Trapunto quilting isn't something that everyone will like to do, nor is it strictly for girls!

SOME GUIDELINES FOR JUDGING TRAPUNTO WORK

There are no published standards established for judging raised work, but the following parameters have been outlined by Elizabeth Zweil, a judge of statewide needlecraft contests sponsored by the Federated Women's Club of New Jersey. Similar judging systems are used by other state and regional craft councils and other organizations. These suggestions are offered as a guideline for both quilters and judges who have not yet established their own parameters for raised quilting.

The major considerations in judging a raised piece on pre-designed fabric are:

1. Workmanship.
2. Suitability of design to quilting.
3. Originality in quilting and raising design.
4. Suitability of picture frame or mounting or pillow backing.
5. Finishing.

The considerations in judging original design work on solid fabric are:

1. Workmanship.
2. Suitability of design to the fabric.
3. Originality of design.
4. Suitability of picture frame or pillow backing.
5. Finishing.

Judging in the New Jersey F.W.C. is done on a point basis. Over 50 percent of the points can be won for workmanship, which Mrs. Zweil defines as a "certain uniformity of stitches and evenness in following the lines of the design." The remaining points are divided between the other four categories at the discretion of the judges.

A few suggestions that can help you win points:

—A piece that is soiled is automatically disqualified.

—You are not required to do your own framing or assembling of a pillow, but finishing is a part of the whole and will be considered in judging. Be sure that a picture is well mounted, with no wrinkles around the edges, or that a pillow is completed neatly and filled so as to best show off the raised quilting.

—Judging is done on what the judges can see. Remember, they can't see the back side of a picture, or pillow, but they can see the work on the underside of garments—and neatness counts!

—When stitches are done in black thread on a black background, they are judged by the indentations and shadows made by the stitched depressions—the evenness of the indentations is what counts.

CARE AND CLEANING

Waterproofing

To protect your trapunto pieces from water and stains, spray them with Scotchguard® as soon as they are completed, following the instructions on the can very carefully. Once this coating is on, you can wipe off water and most stains with a damp sponge.

Cleaning

Generally, you should try to avoid using anything but wash-and-wear fabrics for a trapuntoed piece that needs to be cleaned often, because it is difficult to iron a piece after it has been raised. In most cases, dry cleaning is the best way to care for a trapunto piece. If the fill or cording and the batting and/or the pillow form are polyester, there is no problem in dry cleaning.

Washing

If your fabrics, including the fill or cording, are colorfast, pre-shrunk, and will not wrinkle a great deal, you can launder them with a gentle detergent or soap and cold water, either by hand or in the washing machine. If you are hand washing, do not rub hard or wring. If using a machine, set it on the gentlest of cycles. To dry, hang on the line, run through the "cool air" or "fluff" cycles, or stretch on a smooth surface like a washing machine top or the side of a bathtub.

If the fabric will wrinkle, you can use a commercial upholstery cleaner to wash the piece. Pin it to an ironing board or other smooth surface (use pins that will not rust). Brush the suds or foam on with a soft cloth and rub very gently to remove soil. Remove the cleaner with a fresh cloth, and allow the piece to dry, leaving the pins in to hold the fabric smooth. (If a pillow form is left in it, there is no need to pin the fabric down to retain the shape.)

To clean velveteens labeled "washable," wash gently by hand without squeezing or wringing. Put the piece, soaking wet, against any smooth surface. With the nap side up, smooth the fabric, going *with* the nap, not against it. Push air bubbles out to the edges. When dry, a couple of shakes will bring the nap up. (To be safe, make a test on a small piece of your fabric first. Of course, dry cleaning always works!)

Ironing

If necessary, pieces can be ironed very carefully on the wrong side after the quilting is complete and before the raising is done. If, however, the piece is wrinkled after the raising, you can iron out most of the wrinkles by pressing with the tip of your iron around raised areas, right up to the stitching. If the piece has a middle layer of batting, don't iron, but stretch and pin over a stiff backing, and steam it. When you are working with a delicate fabric such as silk or satin, press lightly with a hot iron over a dry cloth. A wet cloth can leave permanent stains on this type of material.

Storing a Trapunto Piece

Trapuntoed articles can be folded over tissue paper and stored in airtight and mothproof garment bags or boxes. Refolding and airing occasionally adds life to a piece.

Pre-Shrinking Fabrics

It's very important that all fabrics be pre-shrunk if they will have to be washed later, and the usual way is to soak a fabric in extremely hot water. A new method, recommended by a graduate of the Traphagen School of Fashion Design, is to soak fabrics in very *cold* water for 15 to 20 minutes, dry, and press.

Trapunto Projects

For each of the projects included, fabrics and techniques used for quilting and raising are listed; however, the projects, methods, and designs are all interchangeable. As we have stressed throughout this book, use your imagination and simply let these suggestions lead you into your own creations. Detailed instructions are omitted as they are described fully in other chapters. Unfortunately space does not allow a repetition of them for each project. All of the projects were designed and worked by Mary Morgan unless otherwise noted.

DECORATOR PILLOWS

Decorator pillows are a great way to sample raised quilting for the first time. They are relatively simple to make and can be made from many types of material, in any shape or size, with any of the various raised quilting techniques.

General Instructions for Making a Pillow

Assembly and quilting:

1. Decide on the size of the finished pillow, and cut all layers of fabric, including top, backing, middle layer of batting (optional), and pillow back, adding a ½-inch seam allowance on all sides.

2. Transfer the design to the top fabric or backing (unless working with a pre-designed fabric). See photo 150.

3. Place the top and backing together; add the middle layer of batting between them, if you wish to achieve more softness in the pillow. Pin or baste the layers together at the corners, around the edges ½ inch from the edge, and around the design. See photo 151.

4. Quilt and raise the design according to the instructions for the particular piece you are working on.

Finishing a Pillow with Welting

1. Use welting made especially for finishing articles like pillows, or make your

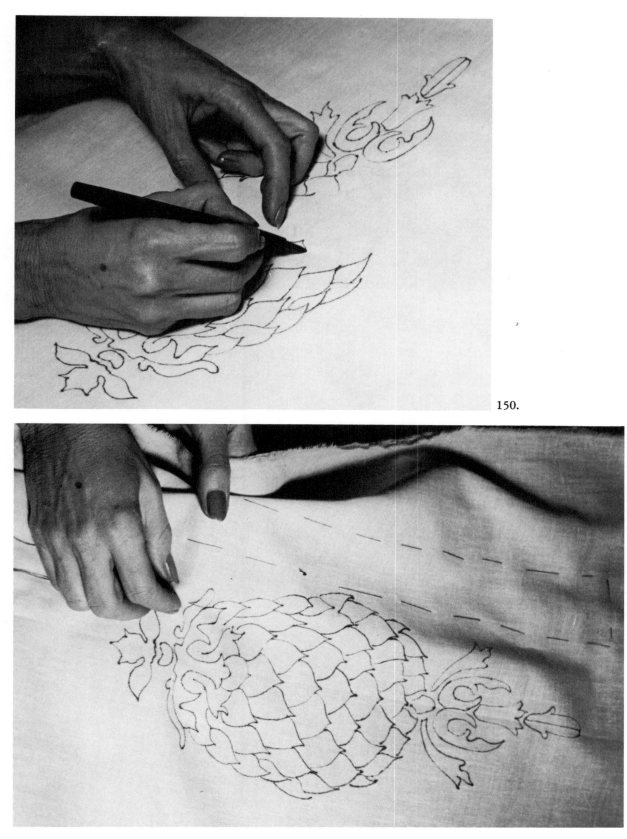

150.

151.

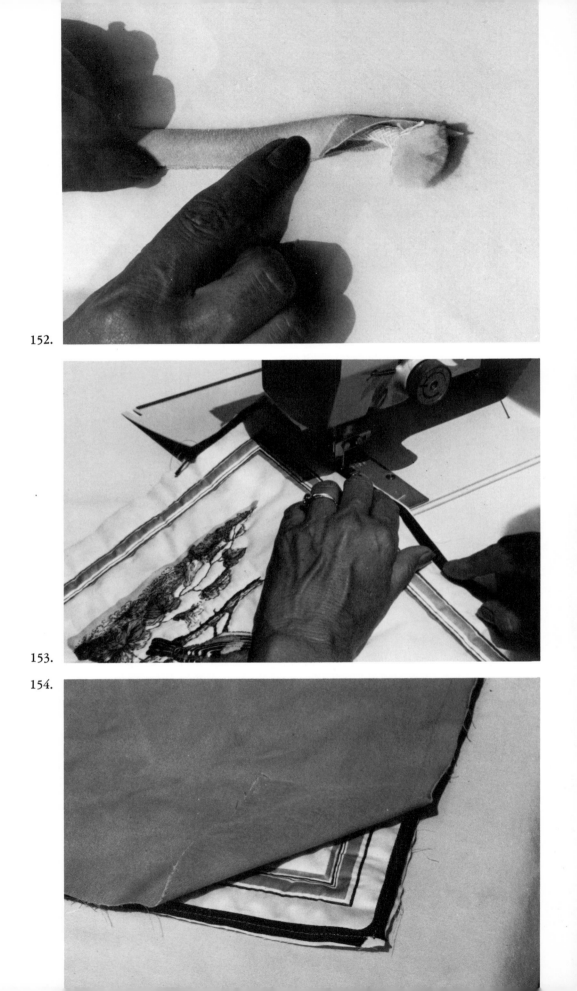

152.

153.

154.

own. Cut 1½-inch bias strips of a material that matches or accents the colors of the pillow. Fold strips over piping or cording, and stitch. See photo 152.

2. Stitch the welting around the edge of the right side of the quilted top, using a zipper foot. The flat edge of the welting should correspond to the fabric edge. To turn a corner, make one or two small clips in the flat edge of the welting at the corners. See photo 153.

3. Pin the right side of the material for the pillow back to the right side of the piece that the welting has been stitched to. Stitch together near the original row of stitching, as close to the rounded edge of the welting as possible, again using a zipper foot. Leave a 5-inch opening at the bottom to insert loose fill. (If using a pillow form, leave the entire side open, except for about 1 inch at each corner.) Add fill, or pillow form, and slip stitch the opening. See photo 154.

Adding a Ruffle

If you plan to edge the pillow with a ruffle or fringe rather than welting, attach it the same way you would the welting. To make a ruffle, cut bias strips of material (you will need twice the length of the perimeter of the finished pillow), and gather them using a long, loose stitch on the machine. The ruffle should have a little extra fullness at the corners, or it will tend to turn up rather than lie flat.

Finishing a Knife-Edge Pillow

1. Omit welting. Place right sides of the quilted pillow top and pillow back together, and baste.

2. Stitch around the edge, leaving a ½-inch seam allowance and a 5-inch opening in one end to insert the fill. (For a form, leave the side open except for 1 inch at each corner.)

3. Turn the pillow right side out, and insert pillow form or fill. Slip stitch the opening.

Assembly of Round Pillow with Band

1. Decide on the size of the finished pillow, and cut top and backing fabrics, optional middle layer of batting, and pillow back, adding a ½-inch seam allowance.

2. Cut a strip for the band, as wide as you want and as long as the pillow is round (circumference), plus ½ inch for a seam allowance on each end and each side.

3. To add welting, place the welting on the right side of the top piece, with the flat side toward the outside of the pillow, and the stitching line of the welting on the edge of the design (½ inch in from the edge). Baste in place. Turn seam allowance under to check placement of the welting. Make adjustments if necessary. Flatten fabric again and sew welting in place with a zipper foot.

4. Pin the band around the edge of the pillow. Continue pinning band to pillow top until the edges of the band meet. Baste in place.

5. Sew the two ends of the band together.

6. Repeat with pillow back, leaving a 5-inch opening near the bottom for stuffing.

7. After the fill or form has been added, finish with a blind stitch.

Pineapple Pillow

The pineapple, as a symbol of hospitality, was used a great deal in traditional quilting. This particular pineapple, adapted from an early American wallpaper pattern, is extremely effective in raised work, though somewhat difficult to stuff because of the many tiny areas to be filled individually.

155. Pillow made of cream-colored cotton velveteen with green velveteen back and loosely woven cotton backing. Quilted in running stitch with silk thread. Individual sections and leaves raised with polyester fill by open-weave stuffing; stems raised with polyester cable cord.

Fig. 19. Design for pineapple body (half).
Match section A with section A in fig. 20 to make
complete design (half pattern) page 62.

Fig. 20. Design for pineapple top (half pattern).

The Green Thumb

Thumb- and fingerprints, with their gracefully curved parallel lines, make ideal patterns for cording. For this project make your own thumbprint on an ink pad and enlarge by the grid method (page 65). To make your work easier, cut the materials in a rectangular shape, rather than trying to work with rounded corners. You can trim the fabric after the stitching and cording are done. Use heavy lines when transferring the design to the backing, as there is a lot of stitching on this project and light pencil lines may rub off in handling. Start cording at the end with the shortest rows and work to the other. An interesting variation on the green thumb would be a thumbprint of natural-colored chamois leather. (You would attach the cord to the underneath side of the chamois top with a cross-over back stitch.)

156. Green Super Stowe®, with unbleached muslin backing. Quilted in running stitch with cotton thread; raised with polyester cable cord.

157. Beige velour top and back, with unbleached muslin backing. Quilted in running stitch with cotton thread; raised by cut-backing stuffing with polyester fill.

Pet Pillow

Velour works well for human and animal figures like this pet pillow, for it is naturally supple and soft in appearance and feel. (If the nap runs toward the back of the cat, it will feel almost as nice to stroke your trapuntoed pet as the real one.) Light-colored velour shows off the raised effect better, but if your own cat is dark, try a matching shade. Or, appliqué a cat of calico or fake fur, and raise it, on a solid background. For easier stuffing, make several large slits in the backing behind the cat's body, and several small ones for the tail.

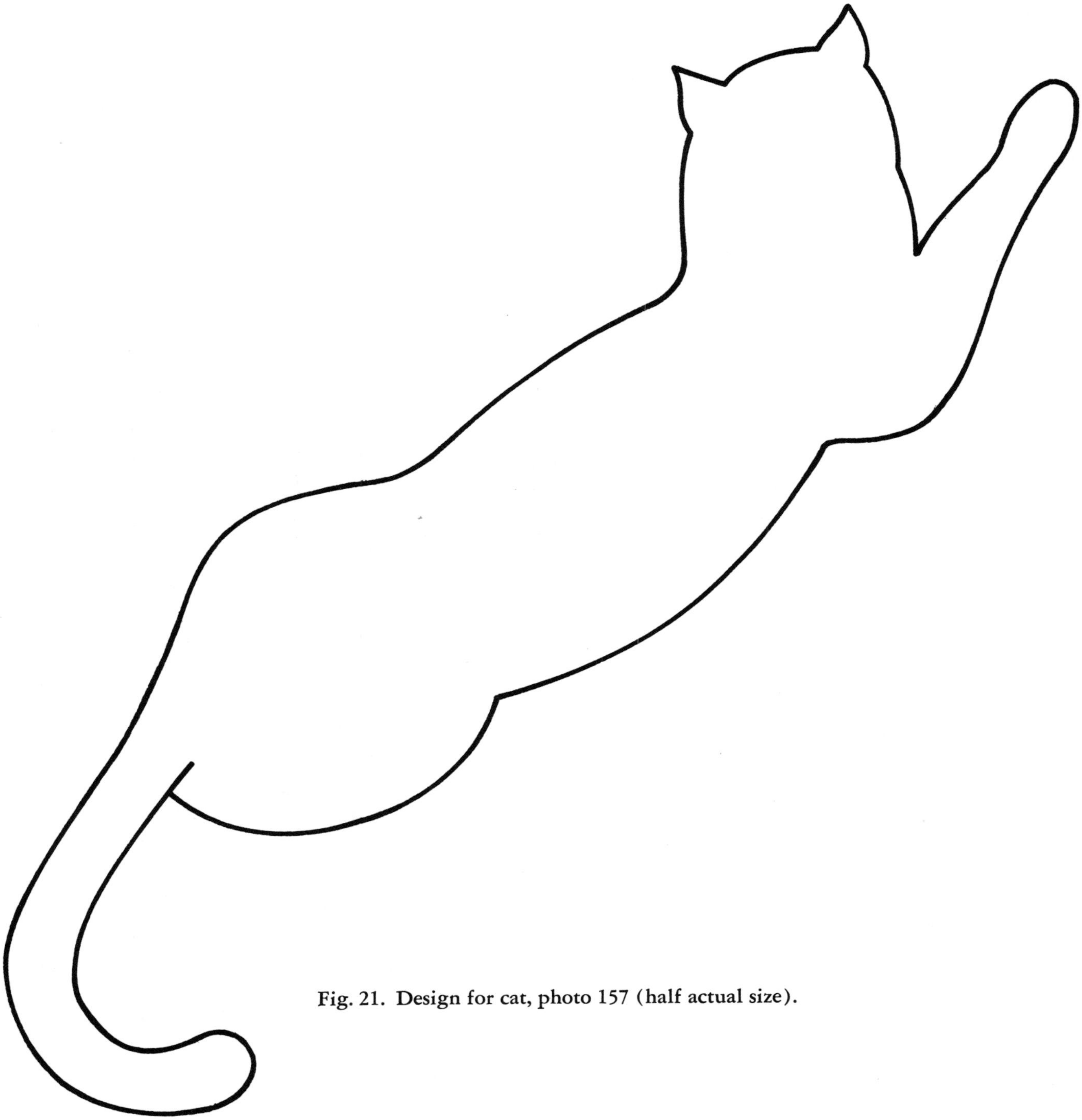

Fig. 21. Design for cat, photo 157 (half actual size).

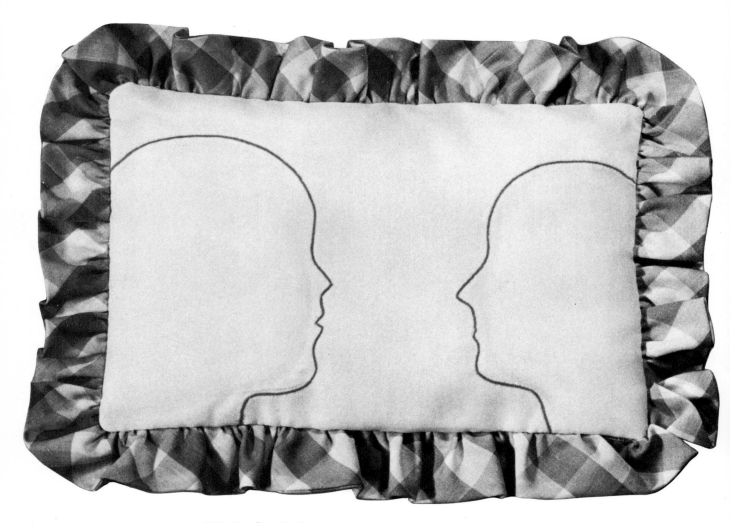

158. Profile of a brother and sister—organza top fabric over white percale, with green-and-white checked gingham back and ruffle. Quilted in running stitch with white silk thread; raised by cording with six strands (doubled) green embroidery floss, and molded stuffing with polyester fill.

Profile Pillow

Here's a new twist on the old silhouette trick: record a loved one's three-dimensional profile in fabric. (This trick works equally well on pillows and wall hangings.) The technique used here is shadow quilting (page 121) wherein the fill materials—in this case both loose fill and cording—show through a thin top fabric. After you have drawn the profile (suggestions for making life-size profiles are shown in photo 159), transfer it to the *underneath* side of the backing so it will not show through the thin top fabric. Add the second line to form a channel for cording $\frac{1}{16}$ inch inside the original profile. Cord first, then fill the faces (photo 160).

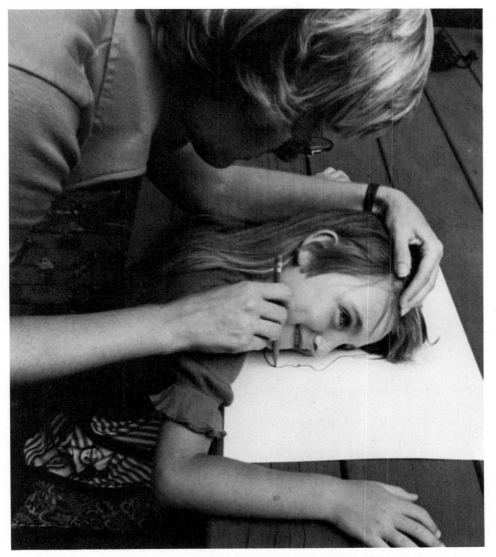

159. To make a life-size profile: Place the subject's head against a piece of white paper and trace, holding the pencil against the face. An alternate method is to place the subject between a piece of paper taped to the wall and a lamp that will cast a shadow of the profile on the paper for you to trace. (The nearer the subject is to the wall, the closer the profile will be to life size.) A third method is to take a photograph of the subject in profile, have it enlarged to life size, and trace.

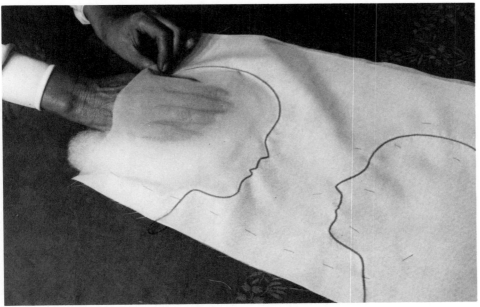

160. To raise the face (or faces), mold the fill into the general shape of the face and insert through the open side. It is not necessary to push the fill into the nose and mouth areas.

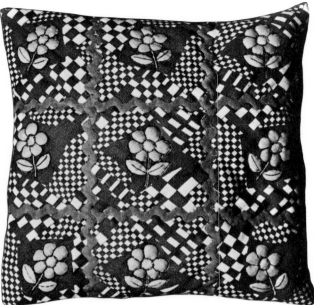

161. "Class Pillow"—pre-designed cotton broadcloth top and back, with loosely woven cotton backing. Flowers quilted in running stitch with cotton thread and raised by cut-backing stuffing (polyester fill). The large rickrack holds the blocks together and hides uneven edges.

Patchwork, or Pieced, Pillows

Pillows can be made in many interesting patterns with blocks pieced together like a quilt. Each block can have a raised design, like the "Class Pillow" in photo 161, or you can use alternating raised and solid blocks, like "Grandmother's Delight" in photo 162. A pieced pillow can be made like a community quilt, wherein each block is sewn and/or designed around a single motif by different needle-workers. The "Class Pillow," for example, consists of blocks made by nine members of a trapunto class. It was designed by a student, Beth Wham, finished by Adelaide Mitchel, and is owned by Mrs. Proctor Ely. "Grandmother's Delight" was made by five-year-old Gayle Frances Wagner.

Piecing the blocks together to form a whole unit is quite simple. Arrange one row of blocks, machine stitch two together (right sides together) on one side. Attach the third to form a row. Repeat this with the other rows. Then place the right sides of two rows together, stitch on one side; attach the last row the same way.

162. "Grandmother's Delight"—made of alternating blocks of pre-designed cotton, with raised designs, and solid broadcloth to complement colors in the design. (Back is of solid broadcloth.) Quilted in running stitch with cotton thread; raised by open-weave stuffing with polyester fill. Dimensions of finished squares: 3 x 3 inches.

Fig. 22. Design (half) for "wedding" pillow, photo 163 (half actual size).

Fig. 23. Design and cutting pattern for chamois pillow, photo 164 (half actual size).

The "Wedding" Pillow

This is called a "wedding" pillow because the fabric is one that is often used in modern bridal gowns. It has a high gloss which produces a sharp, but lovely, definition when raised with cording (compare it with the softer sheen and appearance of the Qiana® fabric used on the bride's cap in photo 207. Made of remnants from a real wedding gown, it would be a lovely gift for a bride. The design was made by the author in the style of contemporary English cording patterns. (Iron-on transfers in this style are available from a number of sources; some are listed in the back of the book.)

163. Deep Luster Satin Peau® (100 percent acetate), with loosely woven cotton backing. Quilted in running stitch with white silk thread; raised with polyester cable cord. Dimensions of finished pillow: 12-inch diameter, 2½-inch band (cut 38 inches plus seam allowance).

The Chamois Pillow

Made of chamois leather purchased in an automotive department, this pillow is lovely to look at and to touch. Because it is assembled somewhat differently than the other pillows given in this section, detailed instructions are given.

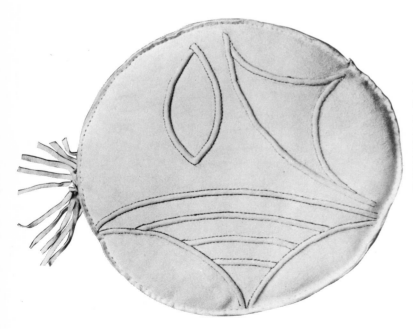

164. Chamois leather, raised by attaching cotton piping to the underneath side of the top fabric with a cross over back stitch (leather needle required). Quilted in rust, brown, and black silk buttonhole twist. Dimensions of finished pillow: 14-inch diameter, 2½-inch band (cut 49 inches plus 5 inches for optional fringe).

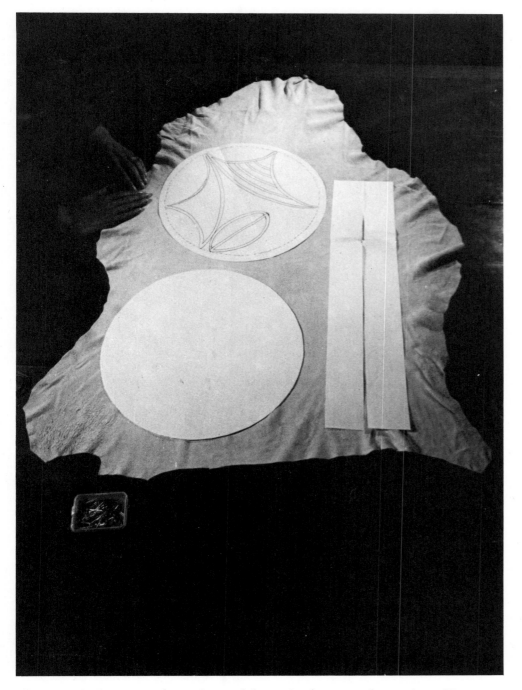

165. Smooth chamois on flat surface and determine best areas for cutting pillow top
and back (avoid thick or rough spots or areas with discoloration). Cut two circles
just slightly larger than the size of the finished pillow, and band (cut 1 inch longer
than the circumference of the pillow, or 6 inches longer if you want to add fringe).

166. Enlarge designs in fig. 23 and make template of cardboard or stiff paper. Arrange on the pillow top and trace. Make inner design lines of the large pattern by cutting down the templates and tracing each succeeding new line. Parallel lines should be ¼ inch apart. Attach cord.

167. Attach the band to the top, with "wrong" sides together, using a long running stitch and leaving raw edges exposed. Repeat with the pillow back, leaving an opening to insert the pillow form or fill. To finish, stitch the ends of the band together. If you have an overlap for fringe, cut ¼-inch strips up to ½ inch from the seam.

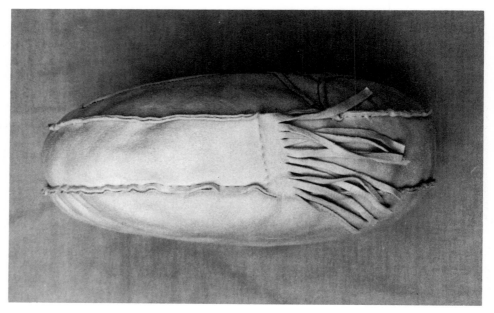

Making Trapunto Pillows from Pre-Designed Fabrics

Using pre-designed fabric is perhaps the easiest way to make a trapunto pillow, since you do not have to find, make, and apply a design. You should, however, take care to pick the right design and place it so that it does not distract from the overall shape of the pillow. Use a window template (instructions are given on page 50) to select the best design arrangement on the fabric.

Pillows can be made from almost any piece of pre-designed material, as long as the fabrics meet the requirements for hand sewing and compatibility with the chosen raising technique discussed in the chapter "Raising the Design," and the design is sharp and clear enough to outline easily. Many of the pillows on pages 147–49 were made from remnants and leftovers found in a sewing box.

To make a pillow from a pre-designed fabric, follow the general instructions for assembling and finishing a pillow on pages 132—35.

168. "Fat Cat," design by Dorothy Draper; cotton decorator fabric.

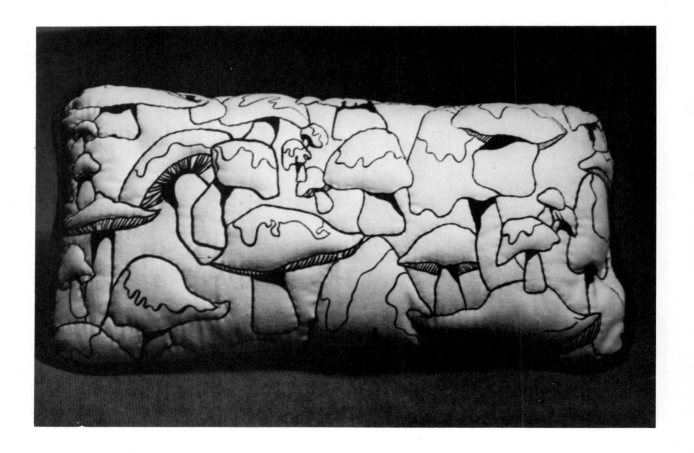

169. OPPOSITE, TOP LEFT: Cotton decorator fabric; pillow by Sibyl McC. Groff.

170. OPPOSITE, TOP RIGHT: "Teal," kit pillow from MM Studios.

171. OPPOSITE, BELOW: Polished cotton curtain fabric.

172. RIGHT: "Salome," design by Aubrey Beardsley, kit pillow from MM Studios.

173. BELOW: "Jungle Scene"; cotton decorator fabric.

TRAPUNTO WALL HANGINGS

It's quite possible that raised quilting was first used on an elaborate wall hanging, rather than a bed coverlet or garment, and that trapunto evolved as much from carved bas-relief wall decorations as from a needlecraft. Wall hangings and trapunto pictures still remain one of the most effective ways to display three-dimensional needle art.

General Guidelines for Making and Mounting a Wall Hanging

Choosing the Fabrics

Since the piece will seldom, if ever, be cleaned, any fabric suitable for raising designs will be fine for this purpose. A wall hanging, then, is the place to use those non-washable, delicate treasures you may find in an attic or at a rummage sale. This is not to say that other fabrics should not be used, but to suggest that here is a place to be creative since laundering and wearing qualities do not have to be considered.

For the backing, an unbleached muslin, or a stronger fabric such as hair canvas interfacing, will raise the design more on the top than a thinner fabric, because it will prevent the stuffing from pushing out the backing too much. This is important, especially if you are going to mount the piece against a solid backing. With this type of mounting, padding that sticks out in the back will lift the piece away from the stiff backing and keep the artwork from lying flat. (If you mount the piece on a stretcher, this is not a problem.)

A middle layer of padding added to a wall hanging or picture gives the piece an overall raised appearance, which may or may not be a positive factor. Sometimes it creates less definition between the raised areas and the background and detracts from the major elements of the design. On the other hand, it can be used effectively on pre-designed fabrics with small, or scattered, design areas that need some definition but not necessarily raising. A simple stitch or two into the padded areas produces very nice accent shadows. (The Persian piece in photo 187, for example, has some small but important designs that were emphasized simply by outlining them through the layer of batting.) Also, if there will be stitching done on a large portion of the piece to flatten the background, the padding can be useful.

Choosing the Frame

Before you cut any fabric, have your frame, stretcher, or mounting board on hand. Working up a design that only a custom-made frame will fit is a trap and can cause unnecessary expense. If you want to frame the piece, take care to choose one that relates to the design. There are many types of frames on the market these days, from simple to elegant, inexpensive to costly, ultra-modern to traditional. There are also a lot of unusual "frames" to be found in strange places (see photo 174).

If you don't have the frame ready before the fabrics are cut and sewn, add a 5-inch margin to the top fabric as a safeguard.

Assembly of a Wall Hanging

1. Cut the fabrics to the (equal) desired size, leaving at least 2 or 3 inches extra on all sides.
2. Transfer design, if working with a solid fabric.

174. Artist Lois Morrison with new work in an old frame. Ms. Morrison frames her unique trapunto wall hangings with old window frames, car steering wheels, rims of discarded cane chair seats, and wooden saw handles. (Photo courtesy *The Evening Post*)

3. Baste the layers of fabric together. (If using a middle layer of batting, insert before you baste.)

4. Do the quilting and raising according to the instructions for the particular piece you are working on.

5. To finish, follow the appropriate instructions below.

Mounting for Framing

1. Cut a piece of backing from stiff material (very thick cardboard, fiberboard, Masonite®, or Styrofoam® are good) exactly the size you want the finished piece to be. If it is to go in a frame, cut the stiff backing just slightly smaller than the inside measurements of the frame. (This is to accommodate the folded fabric.)

2. Place quilted piece face down on a flat surface and center the stiff backing on top of it. Fold edges of fabric over the board. Pull the fabric taut, but not so much that the backing buckles or the raised design is distorted. Use tape to hold it in place temporarily.

3. To secure the fabrics, use heavy-duty thread and sew a network of threads across the back (photo 175). Make your first few long stitches from the center of one side to the center of the other. Next, sew diagonally, back and forth, from one side of a corner to the other side. Go from corner to corner, stretching and easing the fabric to make it smooth, until all corners are sewn.

4. Frame, and hang.

175. 176.

Mounting without a Frame

Some pieces lend well to simpler methods of mounting, without frames (this way, you don't have to worry about size and shape before cutting fabrics). The Persian scene in photo 187 had its own natural border, so the fabric was folded over a piece of cardboard and sewn (photo 176). A heavy brass wire was bent and inserted into loops sewn to the top. To mount a picture this way, follow steps 1—3 opposite.

Mounting on a Stretcher

Stretchers, made for artist's canvases and available in art stores, are an excellent way to mount a trapunto hanging. This displays the design well, and because there is no solid backing on a stretcher, you don't have to worry about a thin backing fabric being pushed out on the back side by the filler material and keeping it from lying flat.

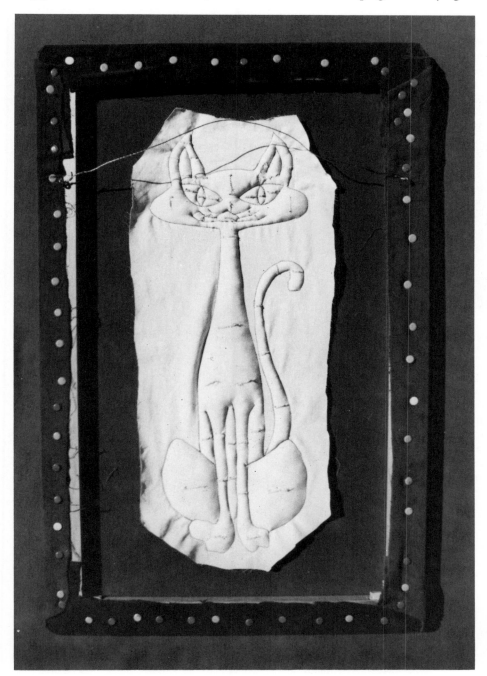

177. "Pussy Cat," wall hanging of red velveteen, by Nancy Haas, is mounted on small artist's canvas stretcher.

1. Place the quilted piece face down on a flat surface.

2. Put the stretcher over the piece, centering the design. Fold the edges of fabric over the back of the stretcher frame.

3. Thumbtack at the centers of all four sides, and then tack around the edges, pulling the fabric evenly taut as you go. (If you don't push the tacks all the way down, you can move them and readjust the fabric to fit smoothly.) When the piece is stretched evenly, the tacks can be pushed all the way in, or the fabric stapled in place.

Matting a Trapunto Piece

A mat is a framelike piece of stiff material (pasteboard, cardboard, etc.) which has a hole cut in it to show off a piece of artwork mounted behind it. It is a very attractive and relatively inexpensive way to frame a small piece of trapunto work, but mats are tricky to make yourself. Unless you are very skillful and have the proper cutting tools, we'd recommend that you take the finished piece to a framing establishment or commercial artist for matting. It isn't nearly as expensive as having the piece framed—the one shown here cost less than $3.

178. Small trapunto scene offset by dark mat.

179. Emerald green satin, with unbleached muslin backing and fiberboard stiff backing. Quilted in running stitch with silk thread; raised by cording (outline and five lines of base) and cut-backing stuffing (polyester fill). Trimmed with rhinestone buttons, imitation pearls, other.

Trapunto Christmas Tree

Here is an all-time favorite, for it includes both corded and stuffed work; it's both simple and beautiful; and it lets you utilize your imagination and individualism in trimming with nice old costume jewelry and "pretty things." Satin is lovely, for it glows as a Christmas tree should; but velveteen in white or green, or woven Qiana®, would also be most effective. Cut a tree from stiff paper (folded in half) for a pattern. Cord around the tree outline and in five parallel rows of the base, and then do the stuffing, starting with the outer branches. Use several slits for inserting the fill, and don't pack it too tightly or it will be difficult to trim. Add trimmings before mounting on a stiff background; and you can hang your tree with or without a frame. If you do frame the piece, choose a frame to fit the style of the tree.

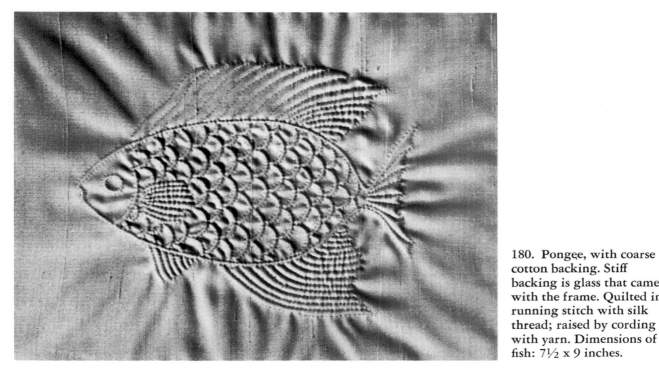

180. Pongee, with coarse cotton backing. Stiff backing is glass that came with the frame. Quilted in running stitch with silk thread; raised by cording with yarn. Dimensions of fish: 7½ x 9 inches.

The Chinese Fish

The stylized fish, adapted from a Chinese painting, is lovely in corded work; however, the small curved channels make it a tedious project. The cording should be brought out of the channel twice in each of those little scales to leave enough slack for "stretching." Cord the inner scales first, then the outline of the body, and finally the fins, varying the amount of yarn for the different sizes of fin channels.

Fig. 24. Design for fish wall hanging, photo 180.

A "Twenty-Five-Cent" Eagle

A good example of how an object already in relief translates into trapunto, this wall hanging comes from the "backside" of the American quarter. This is also a lesson in using odds and ends from fabric to frame. The material is an inexpensive remnant of an expensive decorator fabric, and the frame is an old silver-plated low compote found forgotten, and marked down, its silver plate chipping away, in an antique shop. The stiff backing is a circle of cardboard from a discarded packing box. (It should be cut to fit the frame and then used as a guide to draw the circles— 2 to 3 inches larger in diameter—on the top and backing fabrics.)

181. LEFT: Gray silk, with loose-weave cotton, cardboard stiff backing. Quilted in running stitch with silk thread; raised by cut-backing stuffing (polyester fill) and cording with cable cord. Height of eagle: 6 inches.

182. BELOW: Stuff the body of the eagle first, but don't overpack it (it will look a little flabby until it is stretched over the cardboard). Cord, starting at one side and working to the other. Don't use yarn for it will flatten when the piece is stretched. Small leaf details are raised with polyester fill by open-weave stuffing.

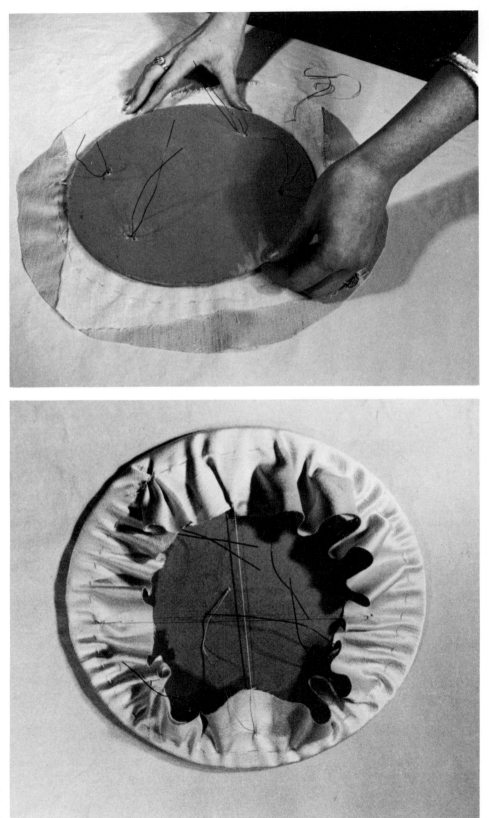

183. When raising is complete, position cardboard in the center. For attaching this hanging to its unique frame, four pairs of tiny holes were punched in the cardboard and 8-inch-long wires laced through them before cardboard was placed on the fabric. Holes correspond with filigree holes in the compote. If you use a "real" frame, you won't need these.

184. Run a strong basting thread around the edge of the fabric circle; pull tight, and it will act just like a drawstring, gathering the seam allowance around the cardboard backing. To stretch the fabric and hold it in place, lace a thread back and forth across the back edge to edge.

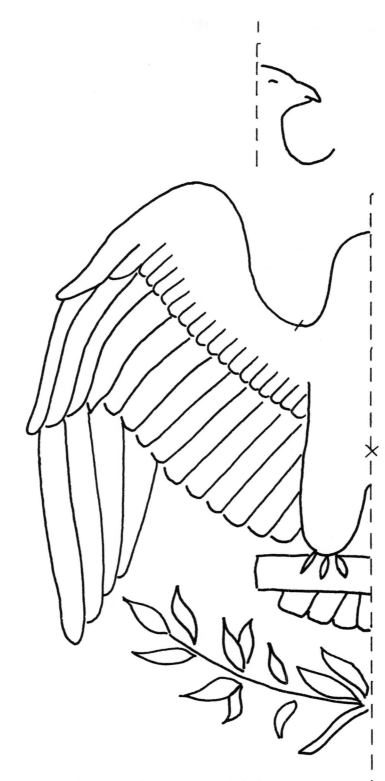

Fig. 25. Design for eagle wall hanging, photo 181 (actual size).

185. Bright orange 65 percent percale/35 percent polyester, with unbleached muslin backing. Quilted in running stitch, raised with polyester cable cord and cut-backing stuffing with polyester fill (large waves at bottom). To attach starfish, two small holes were punched in the center of fabrics and cardboard backing, and transparent fishing line was inserted and looped around body of starfish.

186. Top fabric made of green and blue cotton broadcloth machine stitched together to form a single piece. Cheesecloth backing. Quilted in running stitch, raised by open-weave stuffing (polyester fill) and cording (small top waves).

Accenting a Memento with Trapunto

Raised quilting can be used as a highly effective background for other *objets d'art*—special mementos like antique jewelry, insignias, and natural treasures such as the starfish in photo 185. These pictures will stir many memories and tell real stories, like the "Flying Wings" in photo 186. The wings of a naval aviator, whose life embraced both sea and air, fly between a blue sky and a green ocean.

Let the object determine the design, fabric, and method of raising that will best suit its own lines and concepts; and let the raised work serve as an accent to the design focal point, the memento, rather than as the major design itself. In "Flying Wings," for example, puffy clouds and waves, raised with both loose fill and cord, frame the insignia. The waves roll in from both sides toward the center, further focusing attention on the wings. The cording around the starfish is used more like ground quilting (page 86) than raised quilting, following the outline of the starfish and echoing its shape, with the effect of enhancing and seeming to enlarge the shell. (You could use this technique to create a very striking effect by putting a sparkling rhinestone in the center of a sunburst made of corded rays on white or yellow satin.)

To make a design for a piece like the starfish, place your object on a piece of paper and loosely trace its general outline. Remove the object, and repeat the outline as many times as you like. The channels near the object should be about ¼ inch apart, growing wider as they move out from the center.

Trapunto Pictures

Trapunto Projects
162

A simple way to use trapunto in a unique wall decoration is to frame "pictures" of pre-designed fabrics with raised design areas. All you have to do is to find a scene that you like on a fabric and a frame that will set it off well, raise the design, mount it, and hang it. Here are some examples of very different trapunto pictures.

The "Persian" wall hanging is made from a remnant of exceptionally fine fabric wall covering, which very handily was divided into ten different scenes similar to this one, all perfect for raising and framing. (Another of the scenes was used for a pillow.) A middle layer of polyester batting added to this piece allowed the small secondary designs to be accented by quilting, though not with extra fill. Random quilting stitches made in the leaves of the background tree served as ground quilting and gave continuity to the overall piece. Coarsely woven muslin was used as a backing, and polyester fill was used to stuff the primary design areas. Quilting was done in a running stitch in cotton thread that matched the background colors.

Audubon's *Wilson's Warblers*, silk-screened on cotton fabric, was chosen by Mrs. Leonard Carlson for this award-winning trapunto picture. (Her prizes for the piece included a first in the Ninth District of the New Jersey State Federation of Women's Clubs and a second in the state.) This is a good example of the type of pre-designed fabric that works so well with raised quilting—the design is complex but

187. Persian wall hanging.

188. "Wilson's Warblers."

189. Fire engine
wall hanging.

very sharp-edged and clear, and the natural figures lend well to relief work. The piece was done on two layers of fabric (no middle layer of batting was added), and major design outlines were quilted in a running stitch. Polyester fill was used to raise the larger design areas and polyester cable cord for the stems and birds' legs. Many of the inner details were quilted after the fill was added.

The fire engine in photo 189 is of modern slipcover/curtain fabric of cotton. It was quilted, stuffed, and framed by Mrs. Carl Maple. All quilting was done in a back stitch in black embroidery thread, and the main design area only was filled with cotton cosmetic balls.

TRAPUNTO ON GARMENTS

A raised design, even a small one, can add to a skirt, blouse, necktie, jacket, or other garment the certain touch that makes it unique and elegant. It's quite easy to add a raised design in the process of making a garment, but keep in mind that raising can shrink a piece somewhat and that you must allow for this shrinkage when you cut out the pattern. For a piece with only a few raised areas, add about ½ inch to the pattern on all sides; for a piece that will be largely covered by rows of cording or many stuffed or corded designs, either use a pattern that is one size larger than normal, or quilt and raise the designs on the fabric before cutting out the garment.

Raising designs on ready-made items is also simple. Normally, you can simply add a piece of backing to the area directly behind the design, without taking the garment apart, and quilt and raise with no problem.

190. Mary Morgan in costume designed for lecturing.

Adding a Design While Making a Garment

These instructions pertain specifically to the jacket shown in photo 190; however, they apply to any other garment as well.

1. Trace the design or designs onto tracing paper. If there are a number of separate components, cut them apart so that you can "play" with the arrangement.

2. Place the design pieces on top of the appropriate pattern piece for arrangement. If the design will cross a seam, such as the shoulder seam shown here, place the pattern pieces together, and make a tracing of the pattern area where the designs will be placed on a sheet of tracing paper. Make your arrangement on this paper and then trace the design directly on the garment pattern.

191.

3. Cut backing fabric from the appropriate patterns, and transfer the designs to it from the arrangement in step 2. (Make sure that when the backing pieces are stitched together the design lines will meet accurately.)

192.

4. Cut out the top fabric pieces and baste them to the backing. Stitch at seam lines that cross design areas.

5. Quilt and raise designs, and finish the garment according to pattern instructions.

Skirts

The basic A-shaped skirts—like those in photos 193, 194, and 195—or a straight panel skirt generally show off raised work better than a full skirt with gathers and folds that may cover some of the design. For a full skirt, it's better to use a simple border design of cording than a large overall design. The three skirts shown illustrate three different methods of raising designs on clothes. A full-length "A" skirt pattern (used to make all three) is included (fig. 26); however, you can use any similar commercial pattern just as well.

For a floral print, such as the skirts in photos 193 and 194, the choice of designs to be raised should be made after fabric has been cut so that you can drape it around your body and study it in a mirror. It isn't necessary, or even desirable, to raise all designs on prints like these; in fact, that would make a long skirt very heavy. Choose a few designs in strategic locations so that they will make an interesting pattern and give the skirt enough body to hang evenly. (Avoid raising designs over hips and tummy, for obvious reasons.) It's also helpful to quilt and raise one design at a time, trying the garment on as you go to see where the next one should be raised.

Making an A-Shaped Skirt

1. Enlarge pattern (fig. 26) (¼ inch = 1 inch). This pattern is a size 12; waist 25½ inches, hip 36 inches. Adjust for correct fit. If too short, lengthen it by inserting a section where indicated.

2. Cut top fabric (and lining, if you wish).

3. Cut waistband 2 inches wide and as long as required to go around your waist, plus 2-inch overlap on each end.

4. Sew the darts in the top.

5. Follow directions with each skirt for attaching lining, if used.

6. Transfer design if a solid fabric.

7. Quilt and raise designs, following the instructions with each skirt.

8. Stitch center back seam, leaving room for zipper. Insert zipper.

9. Attach the band according to instructions for any skirt with a band.

10. Finish with hooks or snaps; and hem, unless you included the hem in the raising process (see butterfly skirt).

Skirt 1

This skirt is made of a decorator fabric designed to be used in curtains. It is fully lined with SiBonne, which also serves as a backing for the raised areas. Top and lining are cut by the skirt pattern and attached at the waist. Areas to be raised are pinned, quilted in a running stitch (thread color to match the outline of the design), and stuffed individually. Flowers and leaves are stuffed as single units, with inner details being quilted with a stab stitch after the fill has been added; stems and other narrow areas are raised with cord.

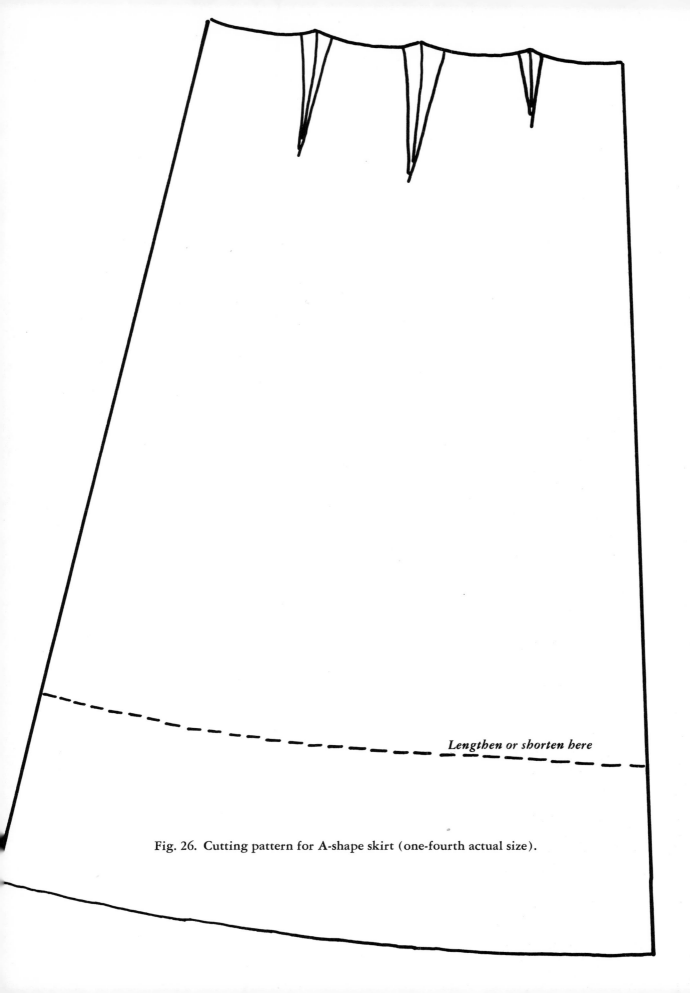

Lengthen or shorten here

Fig. 26. Cutting pattern for A-shape skirt (one-fourth actual size).

193. Skirt 1.

194. Skirt 2.

195. Skirt 3.

Skirt 2

Made of floral print polished cotton, this skirt was cut and assembled according to instructions before the raising was done. It is not lined, so each raised area must have a backing piece (cut 1 inch larger on all sides than the design). SiBonne is used as backing. The petals and centers of the large sunflowers are raised independently; the "mum"-type flowers are raised as a whole. Random single stitches through the fill create the effect of many tiny petals on these flowers.

Skirt 3

A simple cotton velveteen skirt is enhanced by a long, graceful corded butterfly. Skirt fabric and SiBonne lining are cut and stitched at the hem and halfway up each side (photo 196). To add extra body to the skirt, insert a cord next to the hem seam line, and hold in place with a row of (hand-stitched) running stitches on the open side. The design is transferred to the lining at this point, and top fabric and lining are basted together thoroughly over the design area. Quilt with a running stitch and cord, starting at the center of the butterfly.

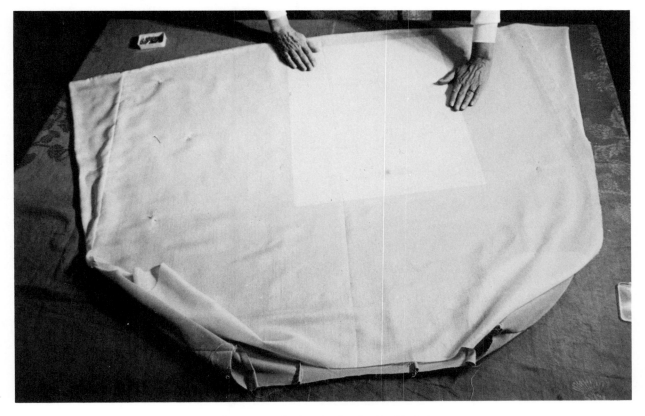

196. After hem and sides are stitched, enlarge design in fig. 27 (half of the butterfly), insert between lining and top fabric, and trace onto lining. Center the middle of the butterfly with a center fold in the lining. Flip the design to trace the second half of the butterfly.

Fig. 27. Design for butterfly, photo 195 (half actual size).

Spider Shirt

A corded spiderweb spun from top to bottom and side to side turns an ordinary ready-made cotton/polyester shirt into a piece of needle art. The spiderweb can be drawn directly on the back of the shirt, using a yardstick as a guide and tailor's chalk for the marking. Machine stitch, making sure that you do not stitch through a channel when two cross. Channels are about ¼ inch wide, and a pre-shrunk polyester cable cord is used to fill them. Since there are no significant curves in the channels, each may be filled with one long piece of cord, coming out only to cross another channel that has already been filled. As to a choice of thread color, if the shirt already has stitching in a contrasting color, try to match that tone. Otherwise, a light thread on a dark shirt, or vice versa, will make the web more outstanding and interesting than a matching color. The spider can be placed anywhere in the web, on the shoulder or sleeve, or on a front pocket. The legs are made with long stitches of doubled embroidery thread for each section, and the body is made of a number of overcast stitches.

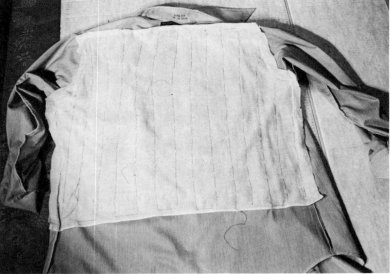

197. LEFT: Ready-made cotton/polyester shirt, with SiBonne lining attached for cording. Machine quilted with white quilting thread; raised with polyester cable cord.

198. ABOVE: After spiderweb is drawn on shirt back, SiBonne lining is attached to inside back at side and arm seams. (Pattern for backing was made of newspaper.) Before quilting, baste lining and shirt together thoroughly.

Caftan

This very elegant caftan has a number of interesting and practical touches. It is made of Skinner's Lute Song®, a lovely, soft fabric with a subtle sheen that is completely machine washable. The intricate trapuntoed yoke and cuffs, which add an important design accent to an otherwise simple garment, are detachable so that the caftan can, indeed, be thrown into a machine for cleaning. The design for the yoke was adapted by the author from a pattern in a modern Chinese rug. It was further modified for the cuffs, and the caftan was worked by Gail Goudzward. The caftan itself was completely assembled before the yoke and cuffs were made. Butterick pattern No. 4814 was used for this caftan, but any similar pattern can be used.

199. Needlecrafter Gail Goudzward wearing caftan she created with detachable trapuntoed yoke and cuffs.

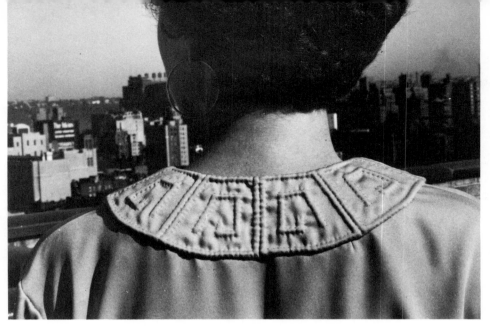

200. Yoke and neck back patterns are adapted from caftan neck facing patterns, enlarged to accommodate the yoke trapunto design. All designs are worked in a running stitch with silk thread; diamond ground quilting is done before raising. Floral areas are raised by open-weave stuffing with polyester fill; borders and geometric figures by cording with polyester cable cord. Neck back and yoke are made as separate pieces, then attached at shoulder seams before hem is turned under and tacked by hand.

To make yoke design pattern:

1. On a large sheet of tracing paper, trace fig. 28 (pattern A) in the top left corner.

2. Place tracing over fig. 29 (pattern B), covering line 2 of B with line 1 of A. Trace B.

3. You now have half of the front yoke. Fold paper on dotted line, with the tracing on the outside. Trace for the second half. (When you unfold the paper, both halves should be drawn on the same side of the sheet and meet at the dotted line.)

4. On another piece of tracing paper, trace fig. 30 (pattern C). Fold on line 3 (center back) and complete the other half of the design pattern as in step 3.

To make cuff design pattern:

1. Trace fig. 31 (pattern D) on a piece of tracing paper, adding a ½-inch seam allowance.

2. Fold at line 4 and complete the pattern as in step 3 above.

201. Cuff pattern is adapted from the bottom of the caftan sleeve pattern. Design quilted and raised as in the yoke.

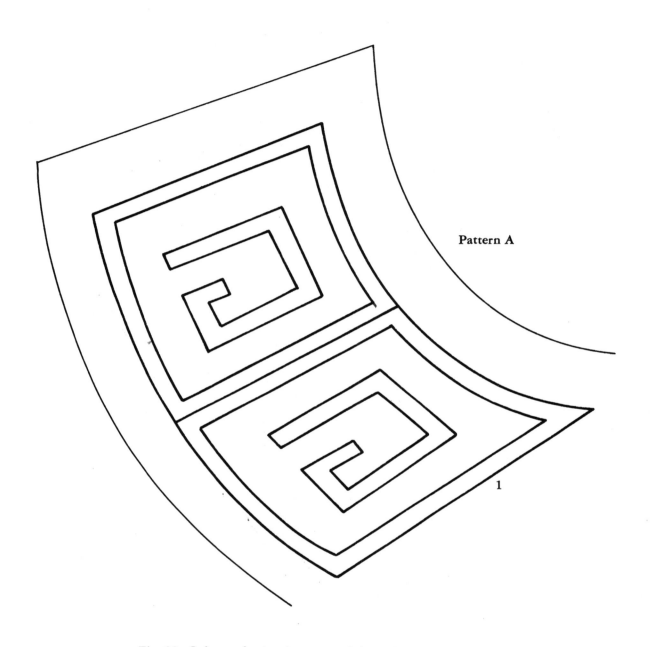

Pattern A

1

Fig. 28. Caftan yoke (top), pattern A (actual size).

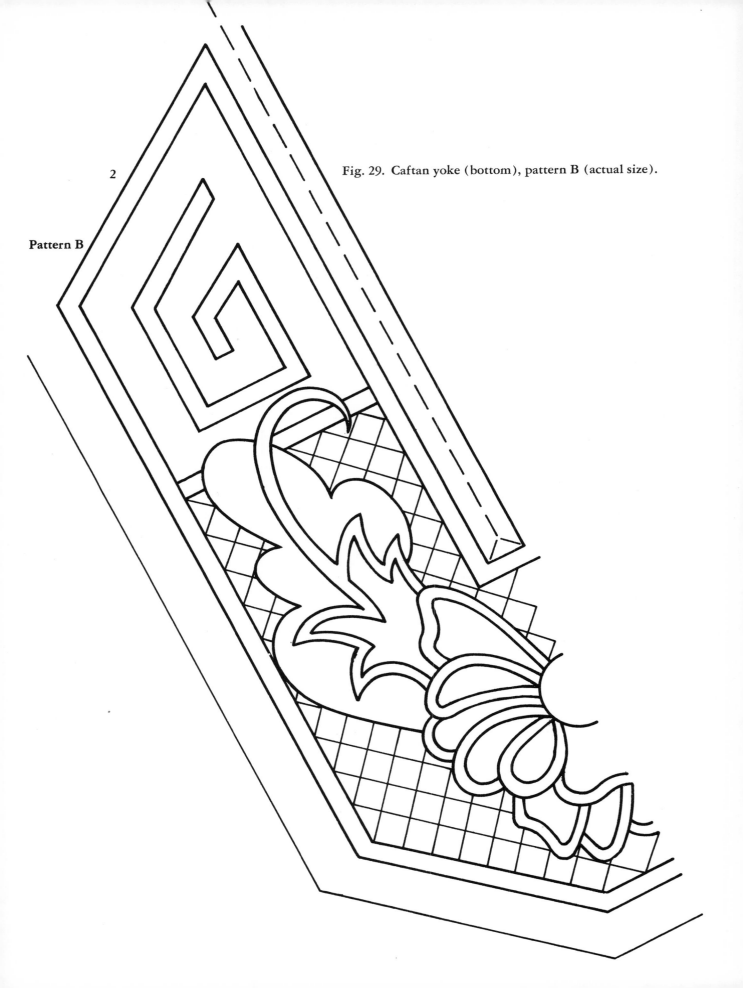

2

Pattern B

Fig. 29. Caftan yoke (bottom), pattern B (actual size).

Pattern C

3

Fold line

Fig. 30. Caftan yoke (back), pattern C (actual size).

Fig. 31. Caftan cuff, pattern D (actual size).

4

Halter Top

Two of the most popular geometric designs in traditional ground quilting—the shell and the diamond—have been adapted for use as the main design motif for this modern halter. Both top fabric and backing are of unbleached muslin, and polyester cable cord was used to fill the design outlines. Any simple pattern for a halter top like this can be used; the pattern here was home-made.

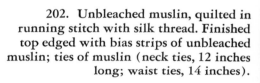

202. Unbleached muslin, quilted in running stitch with silk thread. Finished top edged with bias strips of unbleached muslin; ties of muslin (neck ties, 12 inches long; waist ties, 14 inches).

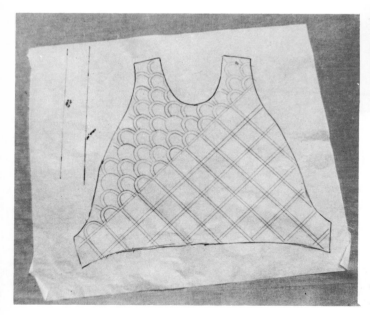

203. LEFT: To make shell and diamond pattern for overall top, trace outline of halter pattern on tracing paper. (Allow 1 inch on all sides for "shrinkage" with cording.) Place design in fig. 32 under this pattern, at the angle shown here. Trace shells and diamonds, move paper and continue until the design covers the whole pattern outline. Transfer this entire pattern to backing. (For one-step transfer, do the original pattern and design tracing with iron-on transfer pencil.)

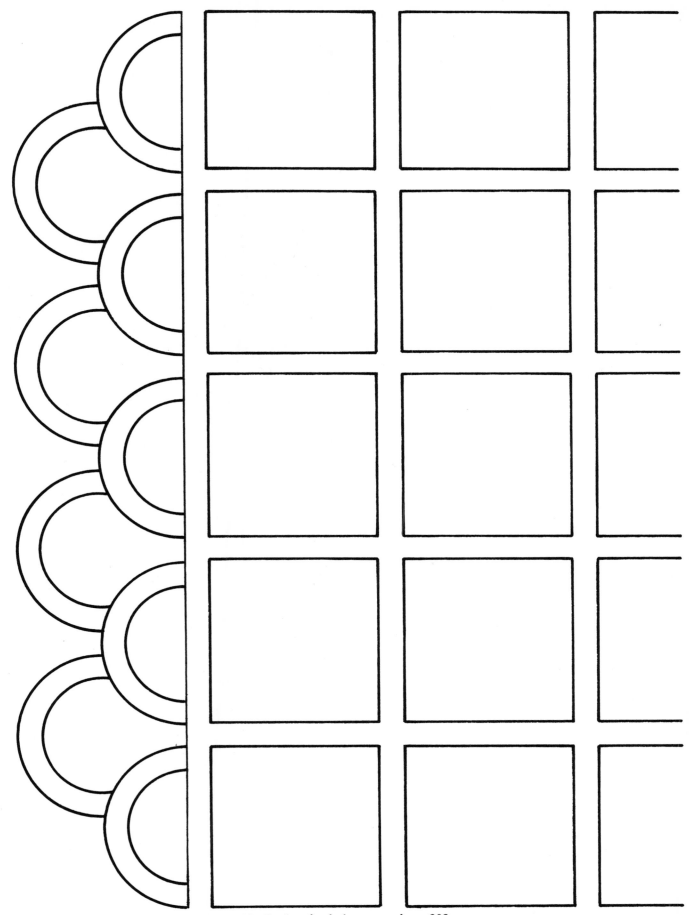

Fig. 32. Design for halter top, photo 202.

Basic "Cover-Up"

The design and its placement, as well as the garment itself, do just what the name implies—covers up. (This design, as a matter of fact, was adapted from a fig leaf "cover-up" on the statue of a young athlete, made by the Greek sculptor Lysippos circa 320 B.C.) Crinkle India cotton is used for both top fabric and backing for the raised designs. A smooth-textured fabric would possibly work better, for the crinkled texture makes it difficult to transfer the designs and equally difficult to see where you have already stitched. The pattern is a one-size-fits-all piece.

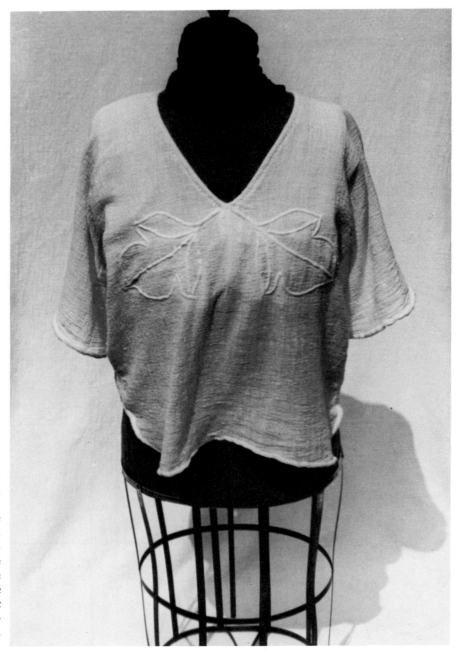

204. Crinkle India cotton, quilted in running stitch with white quilting thread. Raised with polyester cable cord. Neckline is finished by inserting cord next to seam fold and held in place with a running stitch. The bottom and sleeve hems are finished by rolling fabric over cording and slip-stitching in place.

To make the "cover-up":

1. Enlarge pattern in fig. 33 (¼ inch = 1 inch).

2. Cut neck opening. Try on and check side seams for correct fit before cutting sleeves. Cut out four corner sections to form sleeves.

3. Use sections A and B to make the neck facing, which also serves as the backing for the corded designs. Stitch them together and place as indicated by dotted lines. Cut neck opening in facing to correspond with opening in top fabric.

4. Try on facing to establish correct placement for designs.

5. Transfer design in fig. 34 to one side of facing; reverse it to transfer to other side.

6. Place right sides of facing and top together, and stitch around neckline. Clip edges and turn under.

7. Baste around design area. Quilt and cord.

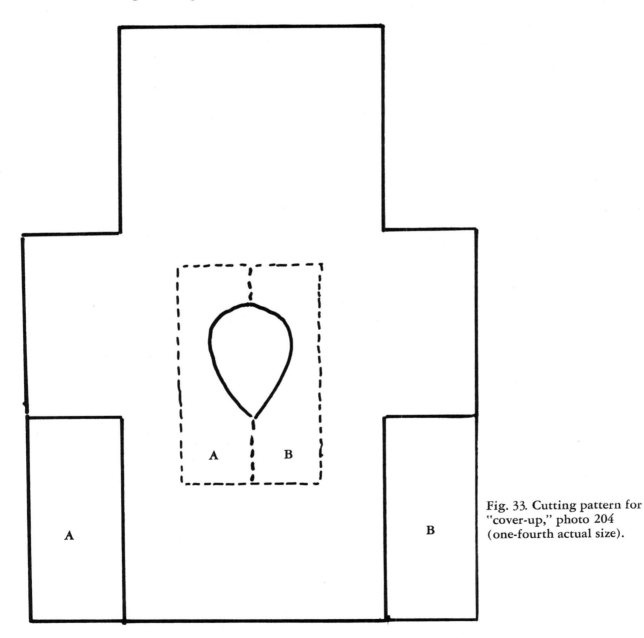

Fig. 33. Cutting pattern for "cover-up," photo 204 (one-fourth actual size).

Fig. 34. Design for leaf on "cover-up" (actual size).

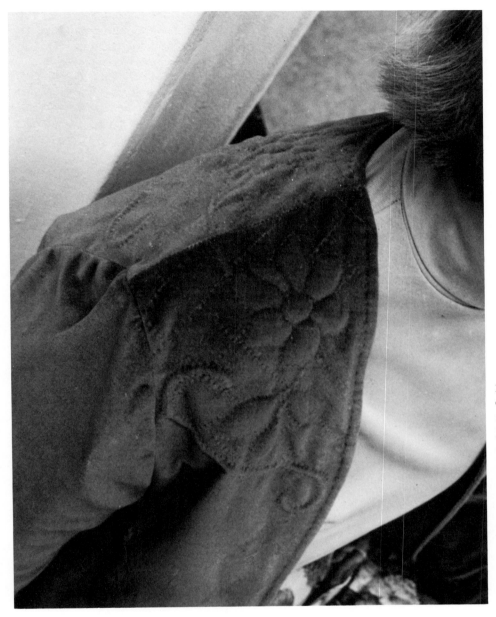

205. Raised floral designs on jacket front were copied from the print skirt in photo 193. Diamond ground quilting was added as a background for the flowers, around the back of the neck, down the jacket front, and on cuffs. Neck and front seams are finished with cording. (If the fabric is heavy, the seam allowance around this area can be trimmed and top stitched, acting as a cording.)

Coordinating Garments with Trapunto Designs

Very pretty, and well-coordinated, outfits can be created by matching a solid fabric garment with a pre-designed one, with a little help from trapunto. Borrow a design from the print fabric, and apply it to the solid one as a raised design. For example, the quilted, raised designs on the neck, front, and cuffs of the velveteen jacket in photo 190 were traced directly from the designs in the floral skirt. Another way to coordinate is to cut out designs from the remnants of the print garment, appliqué them to the solid garment, and raise. The blouse in photo 136 has stuffed appliqués cut from this same floral skirt, for example.

Caps

A standard three-piece cap, borrowed from traditional quilting, can be adapted to a number of modern uses, from a baby's cap to a bride's veiled headpiece. The thirty-year-old patterns given here can perhaps be considered traditional, for the simple lines have changed little through the centuries. Note the similarity of these to the eighteenth-century child's cap in photo 12. Considering the durability of present-day fabrics, the cap you make could survive even longer than that one. The thought that you might be making an heirloom or museum piece for future generations is something of an inspiration to choose the designs and fabrics carefully, to make neat, precise stitches, and to do smooth, even raising.

Basic Steps for Construction of All Cap Patterns

1. Cut backing (two sides and one middle section) from patterns given, adding a seam allowance of ½ inch on all edges of each piece. Mark all pieces with "A" or "B" in the seam allowance, exactly as given in the pattern.

2. Baste backing pieces together, matching letters, and try it on for proper fit. It should fit loosely as raising designs will take up some fabric. Take the pieces apart to attach to top fabric.

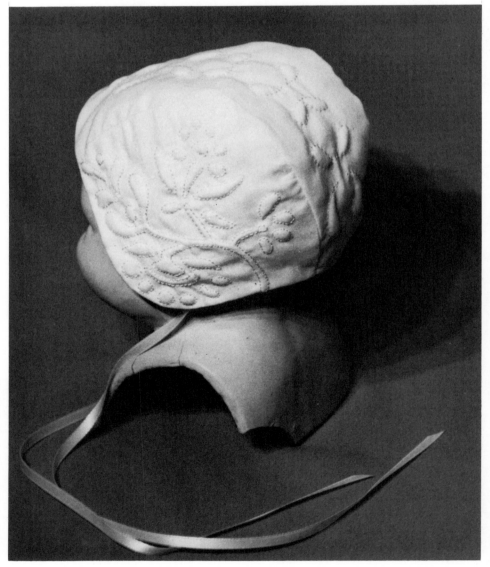

206. Baby's cap of handkerchief linen with loosely woven cotton lining which serves as backing for raised areas. Quilted in back stitch with silk buttonhole twist; design transferred to top fabric with a No. 2 lead pencil. Raised by open-weave stuffing, with polyester fill, and corded with synthetic yarn.

3. Cut top fabric—two sides and one middle section—as in the instructions for cutting the backing (step 1).

4. Transfer designs by the instructions given with the pattern. Baste to backing.

5. Quilt and raise designs, working on each section independently.

6. With right sides together, baste side pieces to middle strip of cap, matching letters and easing in the fullness where necessary.

7. Machine stitch the pieces together.

8. If the hat is to be lined, cut lining fabric, and sew together as for the cap.

9. With right sides together, join lining to hat along outer edges, leaving an opening at the center back for turning. Trim seam, and clip along curves. Turn right side out, and slip stitch the opening.

Baby's Cap

The dainty design for the baby's cap was adapted from the early American quilt in photo 79 and raised in the same manner as the quilt with open-weave stuffing and cording. This cap is made of handkerchief linen, which is soft and pretty, but a viyella fabric (a cotton and wool blend) would give it more warmth and raise as well. Using the pattern in figs. 35 and 36, follow the instructions on pages 184–85 for making a cap. This pattern will fit infants up to six months old, but do try it on for size before you make the whole cap by cutting and basting the backing pieces together.

Fig. 35. Cutting pattern and design for baby cap side panel (actual size). Allow ½-inch seam allowance.

Fig. 36. Cutting pattern and design for baby cap center panel (half actual size). Allow ½-inch seam allowance.

Bride's Headpieces

Both headpieces were made of woven Qiana® with the same simple, traditional floral design; but their appearance is made quite different by the threads used, and the addition of ground quilting on Headpiece No. 2 (photo 209). The design lends itself to both the simple and the decorated versions; and the fabric works well in this application because it has good body, a soft, glowing sheen, is easy to sew, and raises beautifully. (It can also be laundered. But pencil lines are difficult to remove, and care should be taken to make an accurate, fine transfer with a sharp No. 2 lead pencil.)

Using the pattern in figs. 37, 38, and 39 and the design in fig. 40, follow the instructions on pages 184–85 for making either of these caps. All quilting and raising steps are the same, except that ground quilting is used in cap No. 2. The veil is tacked to the bottom seam all around, and small combs are attached inside for holding it in place on the head.

207. Bride's Headpiece No. 1—woven Qiana ® with loosely woven cotton lining/backing. Quilted in back stitch with silk buttonhole twist; raised by open-weave stuffing with Italian quilting wool. Decorated with seed pearls.

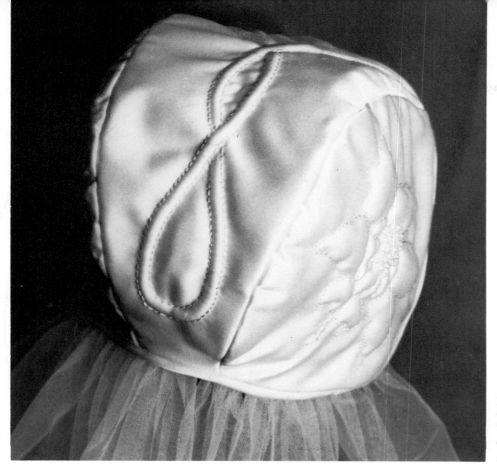

208. Rope twist design used for center panel for both bride headpieces. Quilted in back stitch with silk buttonhole twist.

209. Bride's Headpiece No. 2—woven Qiana® with loosely woven cotton lining/backing. Quilting in back stitch (outline of flower) in silver metallic thread, and running stitch (diamond ground quilting pattern) in white silk thread. Raised by open-weave stuffing with polyester fill.

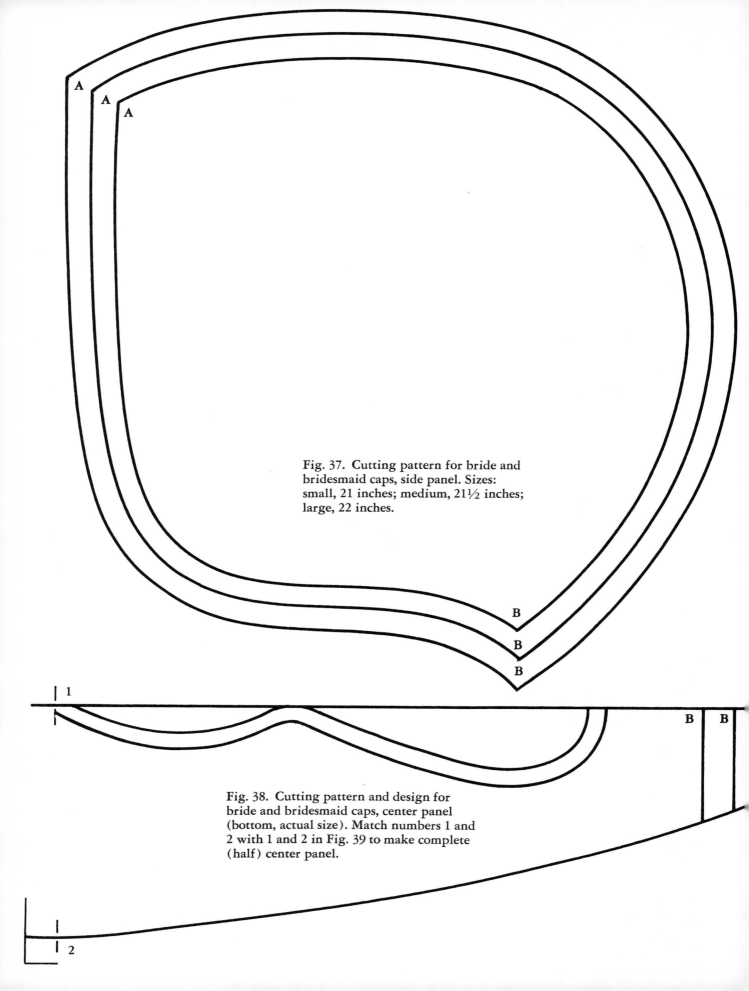

Fig. 37. Cutting pattern for bride and bridesmaid caps, side panel. Sizes: small, 21 inches; medium, 21½ inches; large, 22 inches.

Fig. 38. Cutting pattern and design for bride and bridesmaid caps, center panel (bottom, actual size). Match numbers 1 and 2 with 1 and 2 in Fig. 39 to make complete (half) center panel.

Fig. 39. Cutting pattern and design for bride and bridesmaid caps, center panel (top, half actual size).

Fig. 40. Design for bride and bridesmaid caps (actual size).

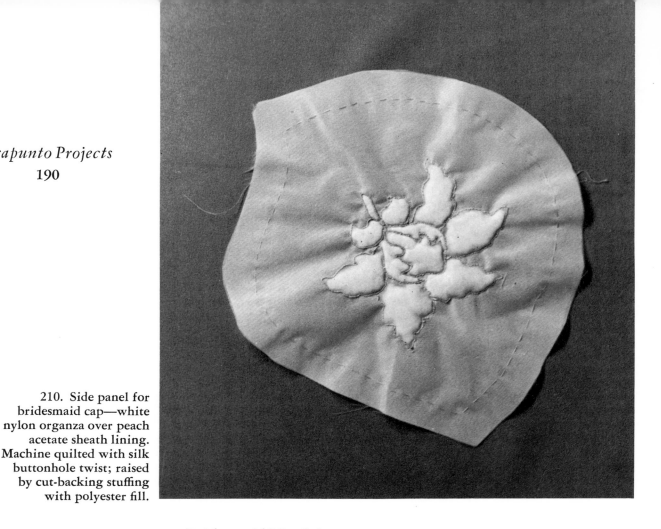

210. Side panel for bridesmaid cap—white nylon organza over peach acetate sheath lining. Machine quilted with silk buttonhole twist; raised by cut-backing stuffing with polyester fill.

Bridesmaid Headpiece

Another version of the same design utilizes shadow quilting effects (dark backing under a semi-transparent top fabric) to create a totally different look for a companion piece to either of the bride's headpieces. (The dark backing and thread can match the color of the attendants' dresses.) The design is transferred to the underneath side of the backing, and quilting is done with heavy silk buttonhole twist (in the bobbin) on a machine. Use a darning foot to allow more freedom in turning the fabric to follow the small curving lines of the flower. When stuffing the individual sections, don't push the fill all the way to the edges; let the backing fabric show through around the stitches to create a greater shadow effect.

SOME HOUSEHOLD ITEMS

Just for a moment there was a temptation to quilt and raise a kitchen sink for a pot holder, place mat, or wall hanging, for it seems that suggestions are given in this section for raising designs on everything but that proverbial sink! This is really a catch-all for projects that do not fall into one of the other categories, and it includes everything from a child's play sheet to hot mitts, from place mats to chair seats. These designs can all be adapted to things from your own home—wallpaper, china, pottery, plants, etc.—or your own original drawings.

Play Sheet

A washable play sheet was designed for a grandchild to encourage quiet activities that would, it was hoped, lead to a nap. It can also be a temper soother when a child is ill. Two highways that wind around over the sheet are formed by rows of cording that hold small cars on the road; and side pockets, formed by folding the corners of the sheet over, make good double garages. The child can create a varied roadway over hills and valleys by moving his or her legs in different positions. And an interesting environment could be added after the sheet is complete by painting or embroidering trees, horses, houses, stop lights, garage signs, and so on in the proper places. (Children can have fun doing their own landscaping.)

The same type of sheet could be used by a bedridden adult for holding tissues and paperbacks. Add a decorative corded design (perhaps the butterfly in fig. 27) in the center, instead of highways. In either case, use fabrics that can be laundered and need no ironing.

211.

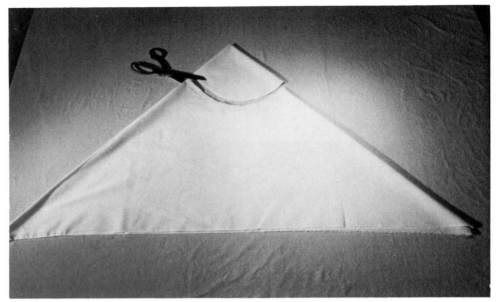

212. Fold a 30-inch square of woven broadcloth diagonally to form a triangle, then fold again to quarter the material. Place point of compass (or end of string tied to pencil) on top center of triangle, and draw an 8-inch arc. Cut fabric on this line.

213. Open fabric and stitch around the half circle; clip edge, and turn right side out.

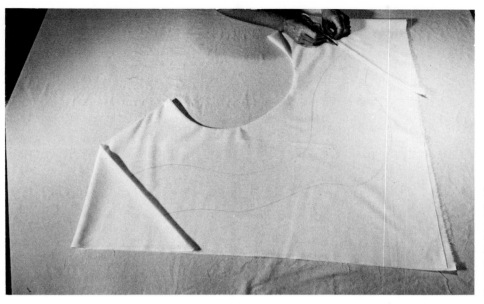

214. Draw in freehand curved lines for center lines of roads. Allow at least 4 inches between lines so cording channels will not overlap. Stop about 12 inches from corners of triangle.

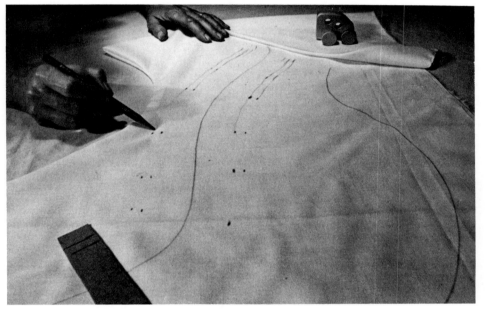

215. To make highways 3½ inches wide, make a row of dots 1¾ inches on each side of the center lines and another set of dots ⅜ inch inside the original dots. (You can make a handy little gauge for marking all four stitching rows at once with a piece of cardboard like the one shown here.)

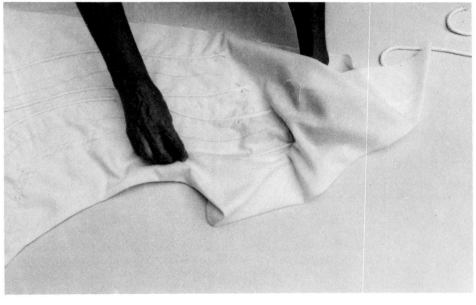

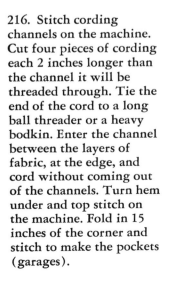

216. Stitch cording channels on the machine. Cut four pieces of cording each 2 inches longer than the channel it will be threaded through. Tie the end of the cord to a long ball threader or a heavy bodkin. Enter the channel between the layers of fabric, at the edge, and cord without coming out of the channels. Turn hem under and top stitch on the machine. Fold in 15 inches of the corner and stitch to make the pockets (garages).

Pincushions

Making a trapunto pincushion is like making a miniature pillow. The basic assembly is the same, and you can use either pre-designed fabrics or solids, and make them in any shape and size. The pincushion in photo 217 is made from a tiny remnant of pre-designed cotton. The hearts and flowers version comes from a small scrap of handkerchief linen. Each one required two circles (for top and back) and a third circle of inexpensive cotton backing, each cut about 6 inches in diameter.

The hearts pincushion design was made from a five-fold star paper cutting, and the pattern for this particular design can be found on page 63. Silk button-hole twist of various colors was used to outline the different shapes to create a very nice colorful appearance. The hearts are done in red in a chain stitch, and the other designs are done in a small back stitch—gray for the diamonds, green for the elongated shapes around the outer edge, and yellow for the butterflies. After all designs are quilted, dampen the piece and press it on the wrong side over a towel. While raising the tiny designs, handle very carefully, as handkerchief linen wrinkles quite easily.

To cut and assemble a pincushion, follow the general instructions for making a pillow on pages 132–35.

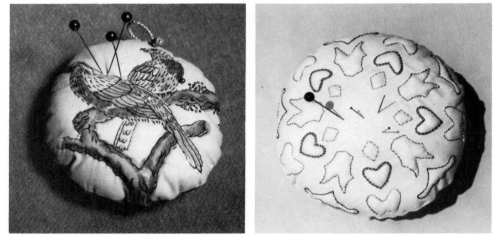

217. Left: **Cotton broadcloth decorator fabric. Quilted in running stitch; raised by cut-backing stuffing with polyester fill. Diameter of pincushion: 6 inches.**

218. Right: **Handkerchief linen. Quilted in chain stitch and back stitch; raised by open-weave stuffing with polyester fill. Diameter of pincushion: 5½ inches.**

Tea Cozies

The purpose of a tea cozy is to keep drafts from chilling the pot and to retain the heat of the tea; therefore, it's generally a good idea to add a layer of batting to the quilted top piece (or between the quilted top piece and an inner lining). Further insulation can come from a lining of wool. Before you make a tea cozy, measure your pot from top to table, and side to side, and check the pattern for proper size. The bottom of the cozy should touch the table (or tray) all the way around.

Rectangular Tea Cozy/Toaster Cover

The pattern for the cozies shown here, supplied by Mrs. Leonard Carlson, can be enlarged to make a toaster cover as well.

1. Measure the teapot (or toaster) and make a master pattern of cardboard or stiff paper about 2 inches taller and wider than the teapot. Cut two side panels each of top fabric, backing, and quilt batting (for insulation), adding a ½-inch seam allowance all around.

2. Measure the width of the teapot, and cut one strip of top fabric, backing, and batting that size, plus a ½-inch seam allowance, for the center section.

3. Pin or baste batting and backing to each piece of top fabric. Quilt the designs, and raise them. In the case of both of these pre-designed cozies, the major designs were quilted and stuffed; and many of the minor details on the side panels and center strip were quilted, but not stuffed.

4. If you wish to add a ruffle, cut a 4-inch-wide strip twice as long as the side and top measurements for each side. Piece if necessary. Pleat with ⅜-inch pleats so that it will have enough fullness to go around the corners.

5. Place the right sides of one side panel and center section together, with the raw edge of the pleated ruffle between them. Baste and machine stitch. Repeat the process on the other side.

6. Stitch folded bias tape to the right side of the bottom edge, turn it under, and hand stitch to inside of cozy.

219. Glazed chintz, with loosely woven cotton backing and broadcloth lining. Padding of polyester quilt batting. Quilted in running stitch with cotton quilting thread. Raised by cut-backing stuffing with polyester fill.

220. Polished cotton, with cheesecloth backing, cotton lining. Padding of polyester quilt batting. Quilted in running stitch with silk thread. Raised by cut-backing stuffing with polyester fill.
Mrs. Leonard Carlson.

Domed Tea Cozy

Four different techniques were used on the four sides of the cozy shown in these photographs to test a new fabric, Silky Satin®. You can, however, make a more attractive and uniform cozy by using the same design and techniques on all four sides, or by using either the corded shell (photo 224) or a diamond pattern on two opposing sides (either will fold for storage without ruining the design) and one of the floral patterns for the other two sides. It was discovered that the fabric is very pleasant to work with and cleans well. It has a soft sheen that shows a raised design to very good advantage. For design transfer, a sharp No. 2 pencil works best.

A word about the four sides: The designs on sides 1 (fig. 41) and 3 (fig. 43) were copies of two raised patterns on the old quilt in photo 79. Side 2's design (fig. 42) is from a nineteenth-century stencil. A ground quilting pattern was used on the third side, but the fabric is so supple and raises so well that the resilient polyester batting, added for insulation, puffs the diamond pattern out in high relief. The design and its small details are almost lost. (If you wish to use ground quilting, use a less resilient batting, such as cotton; or eliminate the batting and insulate the cozy with an inner lining of wool.) Side 4 is a modified shell design in cording.

Treat each side as a separate quilting piece until final assembly, following the instructions below for each. Use the cutting pattern in fig. 41 or any commercial pattern for a domed-type cover. (McCall's No. 8774, with "25 bazaar boutique items," has a food dome pattern which is very close to the one used here.)

1. Make a master pattern from fig. 41 (cardboard is good), and cut four each: top fabric, backing, and quilt batting. (If omitting the batting, cut four wool lining pieces.)

2. Transfer the design to the top fabric, and baste the layers together.

3. Quilt designs, and add ground quilting if desired. Raise designs.

4. Place the right sides of two sections together, pin, and stitch. Repeat with the other two the same way.

5. Make a loop of folded bias tape (4 inches long); fold it lengthwise through the center, press, and stitch the edges. Fold in half, with the raw ends together, and tack.

6. Join the two halves of the dome, right sides together, inserting the tacked ends of the loop at the point of the dome. Trim all seams to ¼ inch and turn right side out.

7. Add a bias strip of the same fabric—or covered piping—to the bottom. Stitch it to the right side, fold over, and hand sew on the inside.

221. Side 1.

222. Side 2.

223. Side 3.

224. Side 4.

Fig. 41. Cutting pattern for domed
tea cozy, and design for side 1
(actual size).

Fig. 42. Design for side 2 of domed
tea cozy (actual size).

Fig. 43. Design for side 3 of domed
tea cozy (actual size).

Basic Mitt

A hot mitt is something one takes for granted, unless it's decorated in an unusual way. A raised design can fill that bill and make a unique gift of the common kitchen mitt. The instructions here deal with the corn mitt specifically, but they would apply, basically, to any mitt, including the one of pre-designed fabric in photo 227.

Work with each side—the back of the hand and the palm—as separate entities until final assembly.

1. Cut four pieces of unbleached muslin (8 × 10 inches is a handy size to work with). Trace the outline of the mitt in fig. 44 on two of the pieces of muslin, one with the thumb on the left side and other with the thumb on the right. (The other two pieces of muslin will be backing.) Cut three pieces of quilt batting the same size.

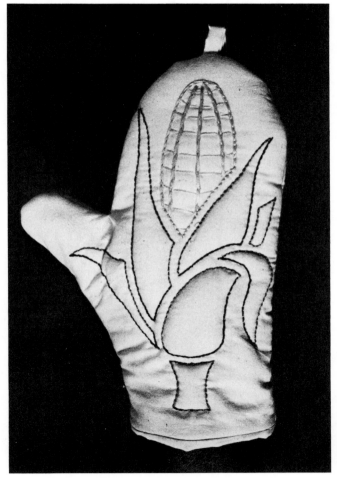

225. Unbleached muslin top and backing (for both sides of mitt), with padding of polyester quilt batting (one layer for back side, two layers for palm).

Back Side (photo 225)

2. Transfer the corn design in fig. 44 to one of the mitt outlines on muslin. If it is to be right-handed, make sure that the thumb is on the left side of the pattern, and vice versa.

3. Baste the top fabric, one layer of quilt batting, and the backing together.

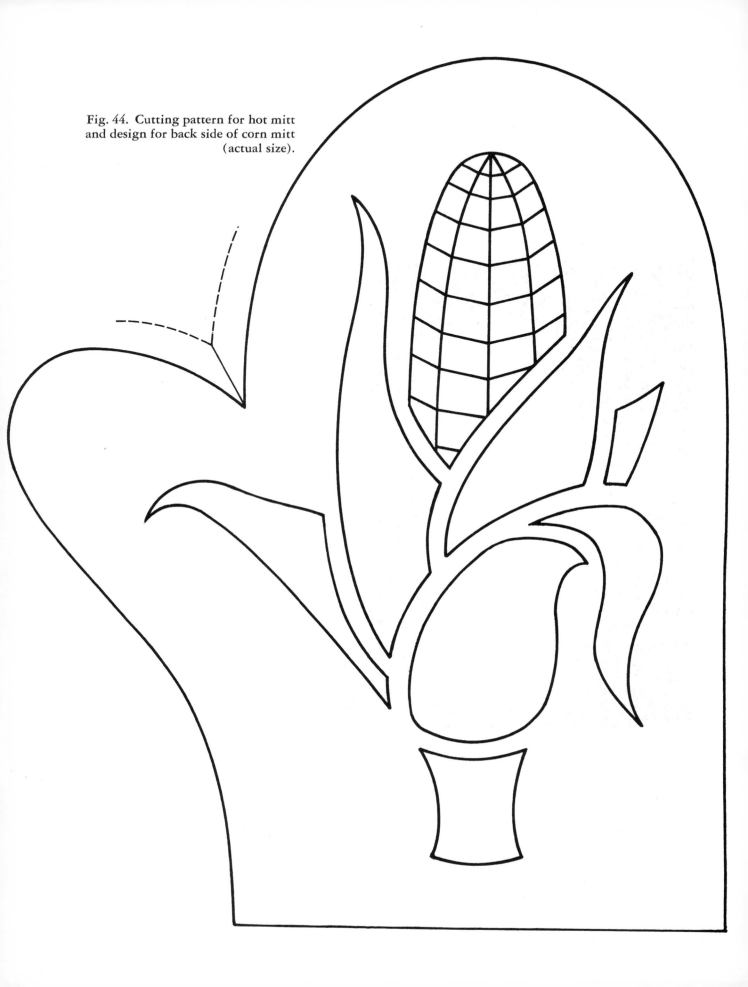

Fig. 44. Cutting pattern for hot mitt
and design for back side of corn mitt
(actual size).

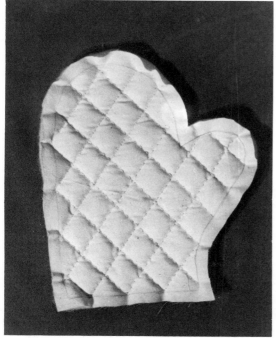

226. Palm side of mitt.

4. Outline corn husks and stalk in a back stitch with three strands of green embroidery thread.

5. Quilt the bottom of the cob (the line next to the husks) with a back stitch in yellow.

6. Quilt the side edges of the corn cob in a chain stitch (yellow).

7. Stuff the cob, husks, and stalk.

8. Quilt details of the kernels. Here a surface chain stitch was used for the vertical rows as an accent (see page 81 for instructions). To give added emphasis to the kernels, after stuffing use a stab stitch (page 78) to go through the fill and depress the rows of stitching.

Palm Side

9. Draw a diamond pattern on the top fabric, using a yardstick to draw the patterns (photo 226).

10. Baste top fabric, two layers of batting, and backing together.

11. Quilt the design with a semi-back stitch, going through all four layers of fabric. (A stab stitch could also be used.)

Assembly

12. To finish the mitt, place the right sides of the two quilted pieces together. Insert loop at top of fingers before stitching. (Instructions for making a loop are given on page 196.) Pin or baste pieces together, and stitch on the seam (solid) line. Clip at thumb all the way to stitching. Trim as indicated by dotted lines. Turn right side out.

13. To finish bottom edge, stitch a folded bias tape or strip of unbleached muslin to the right side. Turn under and slip stitch on wrong side.

Mitt with Pre-Designed Fabric (Left-Handed)

The back side of this mitt is made from a unique piece of dress fabric, and the main design element (the tiger) is repeated on the solid fabric (palm) side; and both sides are raised. The basic cutting and assembly are done in the same way as the corn mitt on page 201; and any combination of complementary pre-designed and solid fabrics can be used.

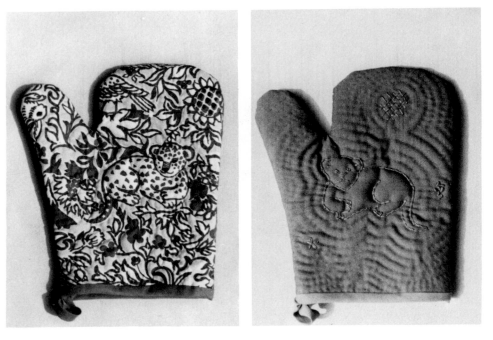

227. Back side—Key West Handprint Fashions® fabric, with unbleached muslin backing, padding of polyester quilt batting. Quilted in running stitch: main design outlined first and raised with cut-backing stuffing. Other details quilted, but not raised (layer of batting gives them the appearance of being raised).

228. Palm side—Super Stowe® with unbleached muslin backing, padding of polyester quilt batting. Main design motif from pre-designed fabric repeated (tiger), quilted in chain stitch with embroidery floss. Other details adapted and worked in embroidery stitch. Wave-pattern ground quilting done in running stitch around all other design elements.

Place Mat

Here's one of the best custom gifts you can give anyone, including yourself. This design was adapted from her own china pattern by Elizabeth Zweil, and the piece was worked by the author. Basic assembly instructions are as follows:

1. Cut two pieces of linen for top and back (standard finished dimensions are 19 × 13 inches) and one piece of backing fabric. Before you cut, however, make sure the material is straight. You can straighten the material by stretching it on the bias; to find a true straight line, pull a thread in the material along the cutting line.

2. Pin or tape the top fabric to the design pattern, and trace. Draw the second line for the border cording about ¼ inch inside the first (which should be about ½ inch inside the seam line). Use a sharp No. 4 lead pencil.

3. Attach the top fabric to backing with basting rows about 3 inches apart. Quilt, using a back stitch on the wheat outline first, and then the border. Remove the basting and press on the wrong side.

4. Stuff kernels of wheat and leaves; cord the stem and border. As an accent for the wheat, use silver thread in a long stitch.

5. Place right sides of place mat back and the quilted top together and stitch on seam line. Leave a 4-inch space unstitched. Trim corners and turn right side out.

6. Press and blind stitch the opening.

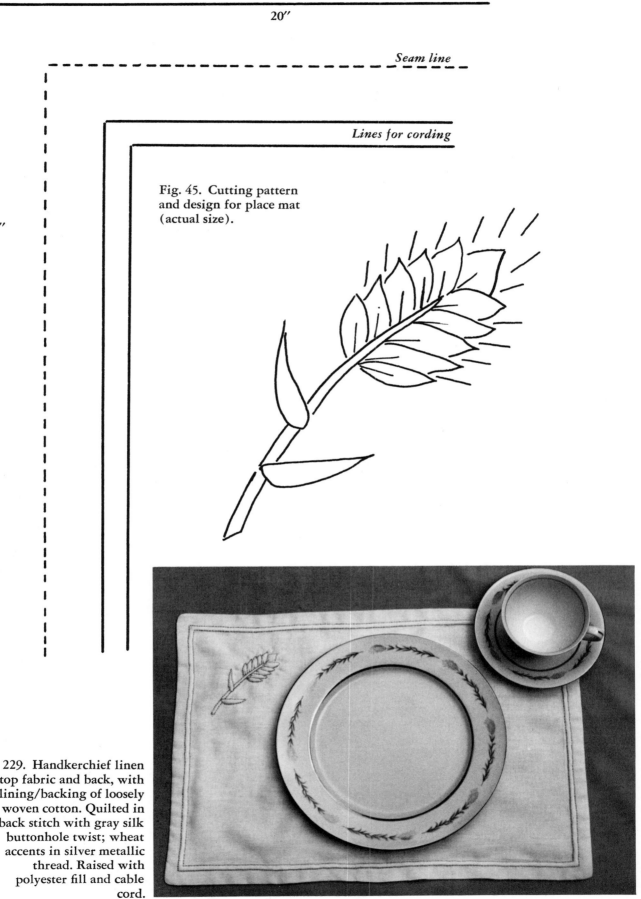

20″

Seam line

Lines for cording

14″

Fig. 45. Cutting pattern and design for place mat (actual size).

229. Handkerchief linen top fabric and back, with lining/backing of loosely woven cotton. Quilted in back stitch with gray silk buttonhole twist; wheat accents in silver metallic thread. Raised with polyester fill and cable cord.

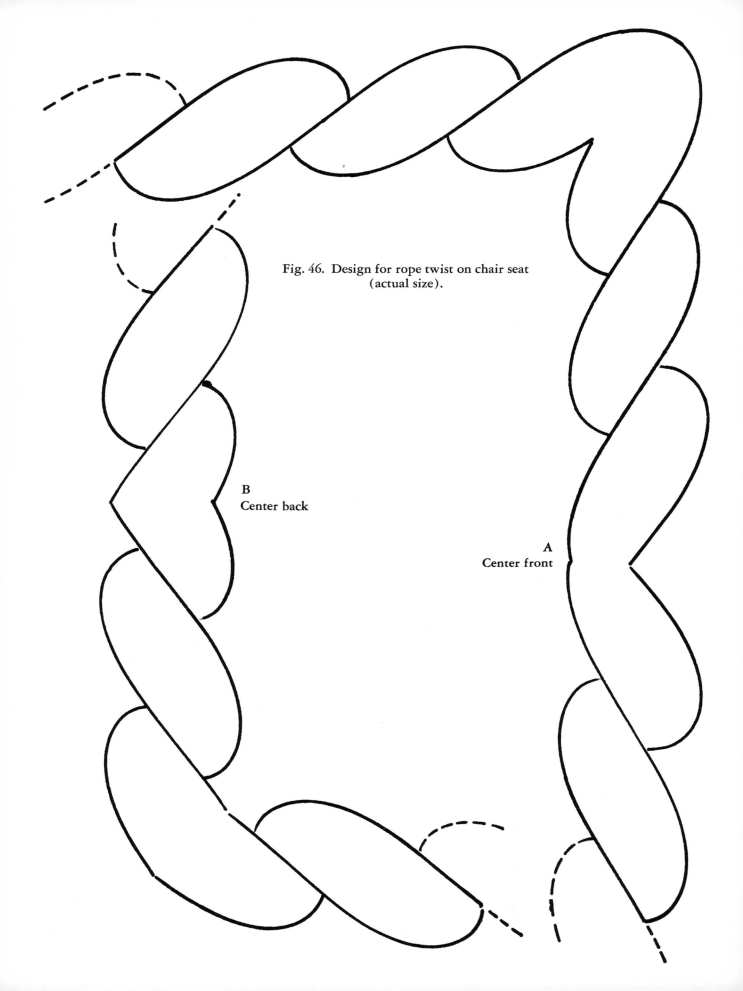

Fig. 46. Design for rope twist on chair seat (actual size).

B
Center back

A
Center front

Chair Seat with Border Design

A raised design can add softness, as well as decoration, to a chair seat or back. If the chair is to be used often, however, particularly in a dining room, you will do well to choose a washable fabric. Certain velveteens, like the type used on this chair seat, are ideal because they are both elegant and easy to care for (suggestions for laundering velveteen are given on pages 130–31).

The design for the chair seat is an adaptation of a traditional rope twist border pattern. Making the original pattern was more challenging and took longer to do than the actual stitching and stuffing—the fascinating technique used to find and turn corners with a border design of this type is described on pages 72–73. (We've given a pattern for the rope twist to simplify matters for you.)

230. Cotton velveteen, with unbleached muslin backing. Quilted in running stitch with silk thread; raised by cut-backing stuffing with polyester fill.

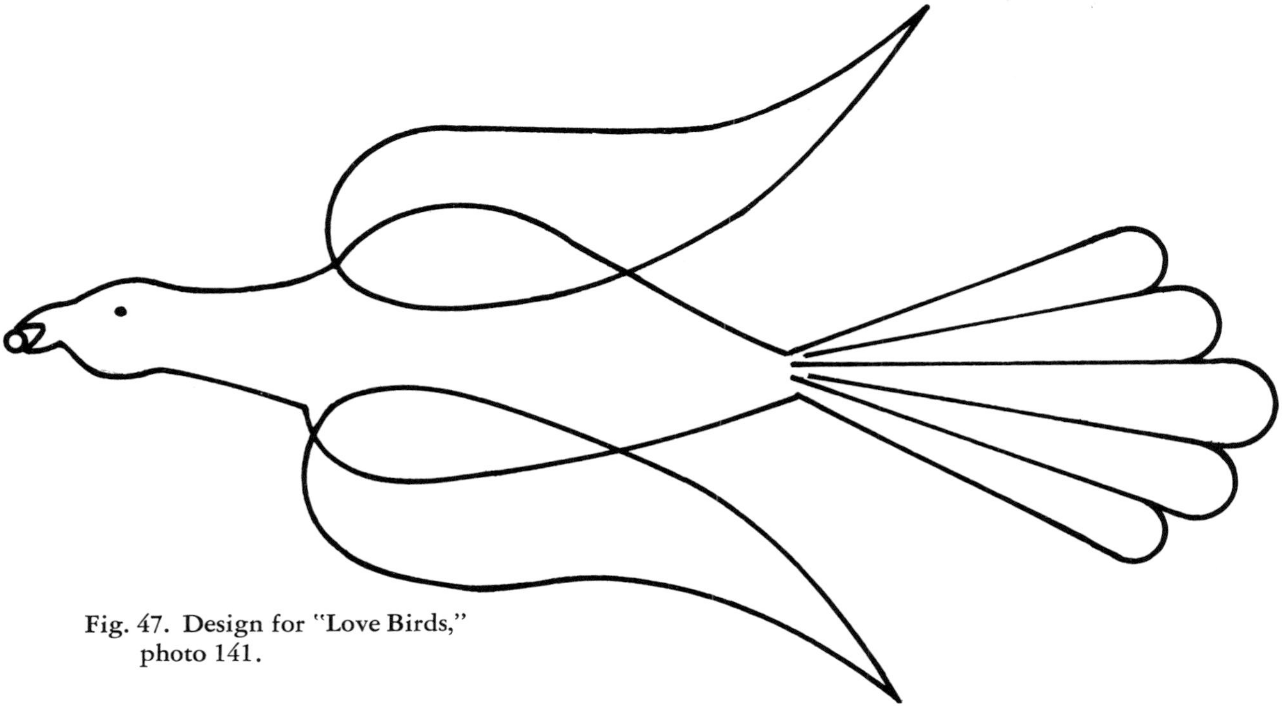

1. Trace the front (A) of fig. 46 onto a piece of tracing paper. Fold the paper at the center line, with the design on the outside. Trace your original tracing, and when you unfold the paper you should have a complete design for the front section (all drawn on the same side). Add two extra twists to each side of A.

2. Repeat with the back section (B) on another sheet of tracing paper. (Note: If you wish to make the design wider, extend the twist sections in the center of the front and back; if you want it longer, extend the side twists.)

3. Put front and back sections together and tape; you now have a whole design that will fit any standard chair of this type.

4. Place the old chair cover on top of the backing fabric and outline for cutting. Mark center of sides and front on backing to guide design placement.

5. Place the backing fabric over the design and trace with pencil or India ink pen.

6. Cut out the top fabric, using the backing as a pattern. Baste top and backing together.

7. Quilt and stuff. To open the backing, cut ½-inch slits in the middle of each twist section.

8. Stitch a twill tape to the edges where the cover will be tacked or sewn. (Again, use the old cover as a guide.) This will keep the fabric from pulling and generally will make a smoother job.

9. Attach the cover the way the old one was put on the chair.

Fig. 47. Design for "Love Birds,"
photo 141.

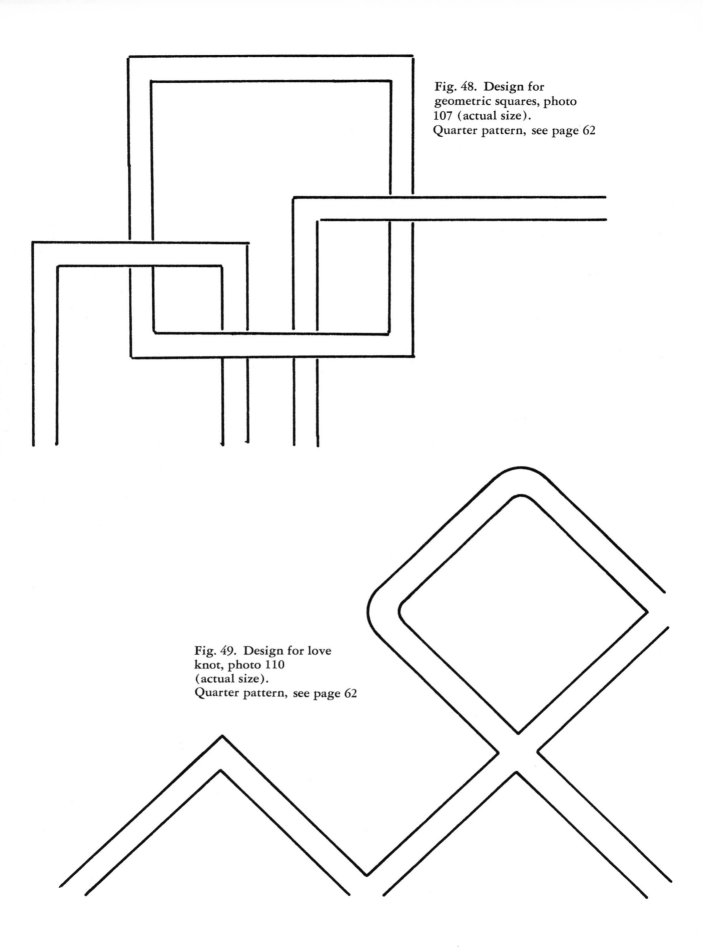

Fig. 48. Design for
geometric squares, photo
107 (actual size).
Quarter pattern, see page 62

Fig. 49. Design for love
knot, photo 110
(actual size).
Quarter pattern, see page 62

Fig. 50. Design for
"LOVE" pillow, photo 95
(actual size).

Acknowledgments

Our very special thanks to the following people, without whose special talents and care it just couldn't have been done: Kathy Alcorn, Marion Batt, Ann Elmo, Gail Goudzward, Kathryn H. Hagerman, Patricia Haynes, Betty Johnson, Marilyn Leon, Anita Prichard, Jillian Slonim, Mary Noel Wagner, and Elizabeth Zweil.

To those artists and needlecrafters whose work appears in this book, and to all of those kind people who provided information, supplies, and other forms of help, go our deepest thanks. Some who went a bit further than the call of duty: Mrs. B. J. Alfers, Marilla Arguelles, Merry Bean, Nola Bencze, Barbara Brabed (editor, "Artisan Crafts"), Sandra Brown, Mrs. Ernest L. Bugbee, Alan Burns, Allen E. Burns, Mrs. Leonard Carlson, Jeanne Coyne, Billie Crumly, Mrs. M. Davison, Michael J. Dorn, Bruce Friedlich, Mildred Guthrie, Evelyn Hackley, Carter Houck, Betty Jeffers, Bucky King, Bonnie Leman (editor, "Quilter's Newsletter"), Sibyl McC. Groff, Ethelyn McKennon, Randy Morgan, Bets Ramsey, Irene C. Reed, Marcia Shapiro, Mahbubeh Stave, Elizabeth M. Wagner, Elizabeth Williamson, Mrs. Randolph Hock.

We also appreciate the efforts of the following institutions in helping us find examples of raised quilting and in giving us permission to use their photographs or to take our own: The American Crafts Council of New York; The Central Hall Gallery in Port Washington, New York; Marileon Fabric Designs of Richmond; The Newark Museum of Newark, New Jersey, for permission to use photos 13 and 14; The Smithsonian Institution, Division of Textiles, Washington, D.C., for permission to use photos 15, 16, 17, 18, and 19; The Victoria and Albert Museum of London, for permission to use photos 5, 6, 7, 8, 9, 10, 11, 12, and 78.

Suppliers

Suppliers
212

1. *C. M. Almy & Sons, Inc.
37 Purchase Street
Rye, New York 10580

Metallic threads, silk threads

2. Marilla Arguelles
484 State Street
Brooklyn, New York 11217

Quilting, trapunto classes,
custom quilting and textile arts

3. Virginia Avery
The Great Sewciety
731 King Street
Port Chester, New York 10573

Quilting and trapunto classes

4. Bartlettyarns, Inc.
Harmony, Maine 04942

Wools, yarn, wool batting

5. *Black Sheep Weaving &
Craft Supply
315 S.W. Third Street
Corvallis, Oregon 97330

Wool batting, quilting hoops,
cotton fabrics, needles, wax, cord

6. *Dick Blick
P.O. Box 1267
Galesburg, Illinois 61401

Frames, muslin, fabrics, bodkins,
cording, wax

7. Boston Center for Adult Education
5 Commonwealth Avenue
Boston, Massachusetts 02116

Quilting, trapunto, and design-making
classes

8. Wm. Briggs & Co., Ltd.
Bromley Cross
Bolton, Lancashire, BL7 9PA
England

Design transfers

9. Brooklyn College School of
General Studies
Adult Education Program
Bedford Avenue and Avenue H
Brooklyn, New York 11210

Quilting and trapunto classes

10. CCM Arts & Crafts, Inc.
9520 Baltimore Avenue
College Park, Maryland 20740

Unbleached muslin

11. Claytons'
Palmer Square
Princeton, New Jersey 08540

Fabrics, threads, cording

12. Colonial Patterns, Inc.
1243 Swift Street
North Kansas City, Missouri 64116

Iron-on transfers, transfer pencils,
quilt patterns, pre-cut quilt kits

13. Contemporary Quilts
5305 Denwood Avenue
Memphis, Tennessee 38117

Patterns, kits, custom quilts and
designs, needles, thread, frames,
polyester batting, appliqué patterns

* Suppliers with catalogues

14. Crompton Mill End Store
12th Street
Waynesboro, Virginia 22980

Velvets, velveteens, corduroys

15. Billie L. Crumly
391 Chapman Drive
Marietta, Georgia 30062

Quilting and trapunto classes, frames

16. *The Edison Institute
Adult Education Division
Greenfield Village
Dearborn, Michigan 48121

Quilting and trapunto classes

17. *The Fabric Shop
1601-09 E. Central
Wichita, Kansas 67214

Top and backing fabrics

18. Fairfield Processing Corp.
88 Rose Hill Avenue
P.O. Drawer 1330
Danbury, Connecticut 06810

Poly-fil® brand polyester batting,
fill, and pillow forms

19. Louis Grosse Ltd.
36 Manchester Street
London W1M SPE
England

Braid, fringes, metallic threads,
cord, silk threads

20. Harrods Ltd.
Knightsbridge
London SW1X 7XL
England

Quilting wool, designs, embroidery
patterns, transfers, templates,
bodkins, beeswax, tracing wheels
and paper

21. *Herrscher's, Inc.
Hoover Road
Stevens Point, Wisconsin 55481

Fill, templates, patterns, threads,
notions, scissors

22. Bonnie Johnson
Box 329
Pluchemin, New Jersey 07978

Quilting and trapunto classes

23. *Ladies Art Co.
P.O. Box 1516
St. Louis, Missouri 63100

Quilt patterns, appliqués

24. Jack Lenor Larsen, Inc.
232 E. 59th Street
New York, New York 10022

Unusual fabrics—wools, linens,
cottons, synthetics

25. Marilyn Leon
Marileon's Fabric Designs
2519 East Franklin
Richmond, Virginia 23233

Quilting and trapunto classes, custom
quilting, and textile art

26. John Lewis & Co. Ltd.
Oxford Street
London W1A 1EX
England

Fabrics, backing, threads, cord,
needles, scissors, other accessories

27. Liberty & Co. Ltd.
Regent Street
London W1R 6AH
England

Cottons, silk, wools, blends

28. MM Studios
18 South Main Street
Cranbury, New Jersey 08512

Wholesale trapunto kits,
trapunto classes

29. Mace & Nairn
89 Crane Street
Salisbury, Wiltshire SP 2PX
England

General supplies

30. McCullock & Wallis Ltd.
25/26 Dering Street
London W1R OBH
England

Muslin, Domette®, wadding, backing,
cording, threads, needles, scissors,
tracing wheels, marking pencils,
other accessories

31. *Merribee
2904 West Lancaster
P.O. Box 9680
Fort Worth, Texas 76107

Thread, frames, quilting hoops,
fill, needles, backing, bodkins

32. *Montclair Art Museum
South Mountain and Bloomfield Avenue
Montclair, New Jersey 07042

Quilting and trapunto classes

33. *Montgomery Ward
All outlets

Fill, batting, threads, notions

34. *Needleart Guild
2729 Oakwood, N.E.
Grand Rapids, Michigan 49505

Patterns, stencils, frames, hoops,
backing, batting, needles, thread

35. *The Needlewoman
146-148 Regent Street
London W1R 6BA
England

Frames, hoops, transfer designs,
bodkins, needles, threads, Domette®,
quilting wool, other accessories

36. *Old Water Mill Museum
Old Mill Road
Water Mill, L.I., New York 11976

Quilting and trapunto classes

37. Other Valley Quilters
12 Washington Street
Northfield, Vermont 05663

Custom quilting

38. J. C. Penney's
All outlets

Fill, batting, threads, notions, fabrics

39. Plum Nelly
c/o Fannie Mennen
Rising Fawn, Georgia 30738

Prints, original designs

40. The Quilt Enthusiast
c/o Georgia Feasel
27 Pasadena Dr.
Rochester, New York 14606

Listing of quilting supply sources,
designs, patterns

41. *Quilts & Other Comforts
Leman Publications
Box 394
Wheatridge, Colorado 80033

Needles, thread, stencils, stencil kits,
frames, fill, batting, hoops, muslin,
templates, graph paper, designs,
finger guards

42. *Christine Riley
53 Barclay Street
Stonehaven, Kincardineshire AB3 2AR
England

Quilting wool, muslin, linens, threads,
Domette®, transfers, templates, frames,
hoops, needles, other accessories

43. *Rochester Museum and
        Science Center
657 East Avenue
Rochester, New York 14603

Quilting and trapunto classes

44. Royal School of Needlework
25 Princes Gate
London SW7 England

Quilting wool, linens, embroidery
threads, quilting and trapunto classes

45. Cindy Ruprecht
Frog Hollow Craft Center
Middlebury, Vermont 05770

Quilting and trapunto classes

46. *Sears, Roebuck & Co.
All outlets

Fill, batting, frames, hoops, threads,
notions, fabrics

47. Sewmakers, Inc.
1619 Grand Avenue
Baldwin, New York 11510

Graph paper

48. Singer Sewing Center
30 Rockefeller Plaza
New York, New York 10020
(other outlets)

Fabrics, notions, threads

49. *Stearns & Foster Co.
The Creative Quilting Center
11750 Chesterdale Road
Cincinatti, Ohio 45246

Cotton and polyester fill and batting
(Mountain Mist® brand),
Mountain Mist® quilt designs,
directions for making frames

50. Stonehenge Mill Store
134 Sand Park Road
Industrial Village
Cedar Grove, New Jersey 07009

Fabrics, especially curtain and
slipcover

51. Taylor Bedding Mfg. Co.
P.O. Box 979
Taylor, Texas 76574

Morning Glory® brand cotton and
polyester batting

52. Toye, Kenning & Spencer Ltd.
Regalia House, Red Lion Square
London WC1
England

Metallic threads, general supplies

53. *Warp-Woof Potpourri
514 North Lake Avenue
Pasadena, California 91101

Quilting hoops, needles, threads, embroidery threads, wall hanging supplies, yarn, linen, cording, classes

54. J. Whippel & Co. Ltd.
Cathedral Yard
Exeter, Devonshire
England

Metallic threads, silk floss, specialty fabrics

55. Emily Whitmore Crewel & Crafts
The Greenbriar Hotel
White Sulphur Springs,
West Virginia 24986

General supplies, kits, custom quilting

56. Erica Wilson Needleworks
717 Madison Avenue
New York, New York 10021

Metallic threads, embroidery frames, linen, wools

Bibliography

ARNOLD, JAMES. *The Shell Book of Country Crafts.* New York: Hastings House Publishers, 1969.

BRITTAIN, JUDY, ed. *Vogue Guide to Patchwork and Quilting.* London: Collins, 1973.

CAULFIELD, S. F. *Encyclopaedia of Victorian Needlework.* New York: Dover Publications, 1972.

CHRISTENSEN, JO IPPOLITO. *Trapunto.* New York: Sterling Publishing, 1972.

COLBY, AVERIL. *Quilting.* New York: Charles Scribner's Sons, 1971.

CURTIS, PHILLIP H. *American Quilts in the Newark Museum Collection.* Newark: The Newark Museum, 1973.

CUTBUSH, MARGERY. *Quilting: A Step-By-Step Guide.* London: The Hamlyn Publishing Group, 1974.

DEDILLMONT, TH., ed. *The Complete Encyclopedia of Needlework.* Philadelphia: Running Press, 1972.

Dictionary of English Language. New York: Random House, 1967.

Encyclopaedia Britannica. Vol. 18. Chicago: Encyclopaedia Britannica, Inc., 1972.

ENTHOVEN, JAQUELINE. *The Stitches of Creative Embroidery.* New York: Van Nostrand Reinhold, 1964.

FITZRANDOLPH, MAVIS. *Traditional Quilting.* London: B. T. Batsford, Ltd., 1954.

HAKE, ELIZABETH. *English Quilting, Old And New.* London: B. T. Batsford, Ltd., 1937.

HALL, CAROLYN V. *Stitched & Stuffed Art.* New York: Doubleday & Co., 1974.

HEARD, AUDREY, and PRYOR, BEVERLY. *Complete Guide to Quilting.* Des Moines, Iowa: Meredith Corp./Better Homes & Gardens, 1974.

HINSON, DOLORES A. *Quilting Manual.* New York: Hearthside Press, 1970.

HOLLEN, NORMA, and SADDLER, JANE. *Textiles.* New York: Macmillan, 1968.

ICKIS, MARGUERITE. *The Standard Book of Quilt-Making and Collecting.* New York: Dover Publications, 1959.

LANE, ROSE WILDER. *Woman's Day Book of American Needlework.* New York: Simon & Schuster, 1963.

LAURY, JEAN RAY. *Quilts and Coverlets.* New York: Van Nostrand Reinhold, 1970.

LEHMAN, BONNIE. *Quick and Easy Quilting.* New York: Hearthside Press, 1972.

LEWIS, ALFRED ALLEN. *The Mountain Artisans' Quilting Book.* New York: Macmillan, 1973.

MAHLER, CELINE BLANCHARD. *Once upon a Quilt.* New York: Van Nostrand Reinhold, 1973.

McCall's Needlework Treasury. New York: Random House/McCall's, 1964.

NEWMAN, THELMA R. *Quilting, Patchwork, Applique, and Trapunto.* New York: Crown Publishers, 1974.

Notes on Quilting. London: Victoria & Albert Museum, Department of Textiles, 1932.

PENELOPE. *Quilting.* London: Wm. Briggs & Co., Ltd., 1974.

PETO, FLORENCE. *Historical Quilts & Coverlets.* New York: Chanticleer Press, 1949.

Sewn, Stitched & Stuffed. New York: Museum of Contemporary Arts of the American Crafts Council, 1973.

SHEARS, EVANGELINE, and FIELDING, DIANTHA. *Applique.* London: Pan Books Ltd., 1974.

SHORT, EIRIAN. *Introducing Quilting.* New York: Charles Scribner's Sons, 1974.

Smocking & Quilting. Glasgow: Coats Sewing Group Publication, 1974.

STAFFORD, CARLETON L. *America's Quilts and Coverlets.* New York: E. P. Dutton & Co., 1972.

SWAIN, MARGARET H. *Historical Needlework: A Study of Influences of Scotland and Northern England.* New York: Charles Scribner's Sons, 1970.

WILSON, ERICA. *Erica Wilson's Embroidery Book.* New York: Charles Scribner's Sons, 1973.